As I Lay Dying

Also by Richard John Neuhaus

As I Lay Dying

Meditations upon Returning

RICHARD JOHN
NEUHAUS

BASIC
BOOKS

A Member of the Perseus Books Group

Nihil Obstat: Francis J. McAree, S.T.D., Censor Librorum

Imprimatur: +Robert A. Brucato, D.D., Vicar General
              Archidocese of New York

The Nihil Obstat and Imprimatur are official declarations that
a book is free of doctrinal or moral error. No implication is
contained therein that those who have granted the Nihil Obstat
and Imprimatur agree with the contents, opinions, or
statements expressed.

Published by Basic Books,
A Member of the Perseus Books Group

Designed by Cynthia Young

A cataloging-in-publication record for this book is available from
the Library of Congress.
ISBN 0-465-04930-3
First Edition

02 03 04 / 10 9 8 7 6 5 4 3 2 1

In Memoriam

John Cardinal O'Connor
who called me back

Preface

When I published in *First Things* an article titled "Born Toward Dying," I was surprised and gratified by the response. The article has since been reprinted in magazines, newspapers, and anthologies in this country and abroad, and I continue to receive numerous comments and inquiries about it. People say there must be more to the story, and they are right. This small book is not the whole of the story, for the whole of the story awaits the story's end, which is not yet. But it is much more of the story of what happened to me and how I have tried to understand it, and am still trying to understand it. Specifics vary from person to person, but it is the story of what will happen, and is happening, to all of us.

Richard John Neuhaus
The Day of St. John the Evangelist
New York City

ONE

W E ARE BORN to die. Not that death is the purpose of our being born, but we are born toward death, and in each of our lives the work of dying is already under way. The work of dying well is, in largest part, the work of living well. Most of us are at ease in discussing what makes for a good life, but we typically become tongue-tied and nervous when the discussion turns to a good death. As children of a culture radically, even religiously, devoted to youth and health, many find it incomprehensible, indeed offensive, that the word "good" should in any way be associated with death. Death, it is thought, is an unmitigated evil, the very antithesis of all that is good.

Death is to be warded off by exercise, by healthy habits, by medical advances. What cannot be halted can be delayed, and what cannot forever be delayed can be denied. But all our progress and all our protest notwithstanding, the mortality rate holds steady at 100 percent.

Death is the most everyday of everyday things. It is not simply that thousands of people die every day, that thousands will die this day, although that too is true. Death is the warp and woof of existence in the ordinary, the quotidian, the way things are. It is the horizon against which we get up in the morning and go to bed at night, and the next morning we awake to find the horizon has drawn one day closer. From the twelfth-century *Enchiridion Leonis* comes the nighttime prayer of children of all ages: "Now I lay me down to sleep; I pray thee, Lord, my soul to keep; if I should die before I wake, I pray thee, Lord, my soul to take." Every going to sleep is a little death, a rehearsal for the real thing.

My whole life long I have prayed that prayer when going to bed. As I lay dying, I prayed it several times a day, for in the intensive-care unit there were no windows, and I could see no clock; I drifted in and out of consciousness, and night fell several times a day. Now I lay me down to sleep. Now I lay me down to die. I have seen revised versions of that prayer in which it is added, "If I should live for other days, I pray thee,

Lord, to guide my ways." I suppose somebody thought the prayer should end on an upbeat note to take the edge off the thought of death. But then why mention death at all? Death without the edge is not death; it is not the real thing. The unamended prayer is one of hope for what may be on the far side of the real thing.

The real thing is the ending that we should know, that we must know, from the beginning. It is the ending that we cannot not know, although we can hide from ourselves our knowing it. *Incerta omnia, sola mors certa*—of all things in the world, only death is not uncertain. So writes the great Augustine:

Everything else about us, good as well as evil, is uncertain. When the child is conceived, perhaps he will be born, perhaps there will be a miscarriage. Perhaps the child will grow up, perhaps not; perhaps he will grow old, perhaps not; perhaps he will be rich, perhaps poor; perhaps honored, perhaps humiliated; perhaps he will have children, perhaps not. And the same is true of whatever other good things you may name. Consider also all the evils there may be; for all, everywhere, it is true that perhaps they may be, perhaps not. But can you say of someone: Perhaps he will die, perhaps not? As soon as a person is born, it must at once and necessarily be said: He will not escape death.

The distinction between human beings and other animals is a subject of perennial discussion. It is commonly and rightly said that human beings are the animals who know that they will die. My dog, Sammy II, will die, as did Sammy I before her, but she does not know it. She experiences a series of debilitations and pains, but she does not experience them as a series on the way to an ending. She has a series of sensations but not, I think, a sensation of series moving to a conclusion. For us, every new wrinkle, every creaking joint bears the intimation of mortality. Many years ago I read somewhere that a human being would know that at some point death will overtake him even if he were the only living being on earth. Even if he had never seen or heard about the death of another. Of course that is speculative, but it rings true. Every manifestation of life is specific and particular because it is bounded by the alternative to life, which is death. Death is the clock ever advancing, even if in the far recesses of our consciousness, reminding us that we are creatures of time, that we are timed.

Many have said young people believe that they are immortal, that they will never die. I doubt it. I vividly recall discussing with my teenage friends how old we would be by the end of the century. Fifty-five? Sixty? We unanimously agreed that it was not worth thinking about, since we would all be dead by then. Of course we knew people who had reached the great old age of sixty, but that *we* might one day be sixty was an abstraction beyond our imagination or desire. The young do not think they will never die; many of the more adventurous even court death—in reckless driving, in drugs, in extreme sports that flirt with fatality, in music that pulsates with the titillations of suicide, of inflicting pain and even death on others. This is the dark underside of what is called the youth culture, and it is hardly new. The *Sturm und Drang* movement of the eighteenth century produced literature such as Goethe's *The Sorrows of Young Werther*, which made youthful suicide, or at least flirtation with it, fashionable; and there was a sickly flourishing of the fascinating links between beauty and death among the romantic decadents of the nineteenth century. The artistry is missing, but there is nothing very new about the teenager today who emerges from his lonely melancholy to gun down his classmates before killing himself.

Death brings life to a point. At the end of the nineteenth century, in a sentiment that cannot easily be dismissed as an instance of *fin de siècle* morbidity, the English essayist Walter Pater wrote: "To burn always with this hard, gem-like flame, to maintain this ecstasy, is success in life." The youthful courting of death—half defiance and half invitation—is to live with utmost intensity, to live at the edge of nothing, or of much more. To find out is all. Death is adventure, it is self-dramatization, and it is the ultimate assertion of self, striking the definitive stroke. Even very young children, angry and frustrated by the world's cruel authority, declare, "They'll be sorry when I'm dead!" Far from thinking they are immortal, the young would not be deprived of death. Death marks the boundary of life lived intensely; it is a weapon with which to strike against intolerable limits. Yet we may ask whether death so conceived is really death.

It is commonly said, also by those not embroiled in the sustained melodrama that is youth, that we must accept death as part of life. But it may be countered that death is not part of life; death is the end of life, the destruction of life. To say "I accept death" is to assume that there will be a continuing "I" beyond death. Over the course of a lifetime, I accept many things—disappointments, setbacks, sicknesses, things that cannot be helped. But on the far side of each acceptance, "I" continue. In the midst of his afflictions,

Job asks, "Shall we receive good at the hand of God, and shall we not receive evil?" This in response to his wife's reproach, "Do you still hold fast your integrity? Curse God, and die." Whatever good or evil is received, it is the "I" of Job that does the receiving. But to curse God and die would mean Job acting to annihilate Job. This Job will not do; this he knows he cannot do.

The prospect of his not being, of the annihilation of his "I," is not in his own hands. To even think it, the prospect must be recast in the form of a prayer. And so in chapter 10:

> *Why did you bring me forth from the*
> *   womb? Would that I had died*
> *   before any eye had seen me,*
> *and were as though I had not been,*
> *   carried from the womb to the grave.*
> *Are not the days of my life few?*
> *   Let me alone, that I may find a*
> *   little comfort*
> *before I go whence I shall not return,*
> *   to the land of gloom and deep darkness,*
> *the land of gloom and chaos,*
> *   where light is as darkness.*

In the protest of prayer, Job contemplates his "I" having never been, but the "I" that prays, having come into being, cannot conceive of not being. Even if he goes into death, that place "whence I shall not return," it is still the enduring "I" that shall not return.

The three comforters, who would explain to him the reasons for his suffering, are no comfort at all. Job has heard all these rationalizations before; he would take up his argument with a higher authority. To his well-meaning friends he says:

> *What you know, I also know;*
> *I am not inferior to you.*
> *But I would speak to the Almighty,*
> *and I desire to argue my case*
> *with God.*
> *As for you, you whitewash with lies;*
> *worthless physicians are you all.*

The "I" of Job exists by virtue of the existence of another "I." Job is not a solipsist; he does not entertain the madness that he is the only existent thing. Life is responsible for life, and the personal "I" lives in response to that responsible Life. In Handel's *Messiah*, a passage from chapter 19 is turned into a magnificent hymn of serene reconciliation, "I Know That My Redeemer Liveth." In the book of Job, however, its words are of insistence, of demand, that it *must be* that he will get his chance to argue his case:

For I know that my Redeemer lives,
and at last he will stand upon the
earth;
and after my skin has been thus
destroyed, then from my flesh
I shall see God,
whom I shall see for myself,
and my eyes shall behold, and not
another.

In sum, there will be a reckoning. A day of argument, and of judgment; an appeal beyond the death sentence passed on the "I." The sentence is unbearable, Job insists, because it is unjust. Three of Job's learned friends—Bildad, Eliphaz, and Zophar—had explained to him, at great length, why he was wrong about that, but Job persisted. "So these three men ceased to answer Job, because he was righteous in his own eyes. Then Elihu, the son of Barachel the Buzite of the family of Ram, became angry. He was angry at Job because he justified himself rather than God; he was angry also at Job's three friends because they had found no answer, although they had declared Job to be in the wrong." Then Elihu spoke, but he had no better success. In Job's rejection of easy answers, we find ourselves on his side.

I have been by the beds of the dying who ask, "Why me?" And with those who have lost a husband, a

wife, or a mother and ask, "Why me?" Their death or
the death of someone they love is seen as an injury
aimed at them. Surely the more sensible response is,
"Why not me?" This happens to everyone, so why not
to me? But what, the dying and the mourning persist,
does the fact that it happens to everyone have to do
with its happening to me? The question is obviously a
logical fallacy, for each of us is included in "everyone,"
yet the question does not go away. And perhaps there
is a wisdom in its persistence.

"Good Hamlet," his mother pleads to the prince
dressed all in black, "cast thy nighted color off,"

> *And let thine eye look like a friend on Denmark.*
> *Do not forever with thy vailed lids*
> *Seek for thy noble father in the dust.*
> *Thou know'st 'tis common, all that lives must die,*
> *Passing through nature to eternity.*
> HAMLET: *Aye, Madam, 'tis common.*
> GERTRUDE: *If it be,*
> *Why seems it so particular with thee?*

Why does it seem so particular with you? What is
so special about you that what happens to everyone
should not happen to you?

Claudius, Gertrude's husband and the new king,
has his own reasons for wanting Hamlet to end his

mourning. "You must know, your father lost a father. That father lost, lost his." It is the way things are, the way things must be. Claudius continues:

> *To persevere*
> *In obstinate condolement is a course*
> *Of impious stubbornness; 'tis unmanly grief,*
> *It shows a will most incorrect to heaven,*
> *A heart unfortified, a mind impatient,*
> *An understanding simple and unschool'd.*
> *For what we know must be and is as common*
> *As any the most vulgar thing to sense.*
> *Why should we in our peevish opposition*
> *Take it to heart? Fie! 'Tis a fault to heaven,*
> *A fault against the dead, a fault to nature,*
> *To reason most absurd, whose common theme*
> *Is death of fathers, and who still hath cried,*
> *From the first corpse till he that died today,*
> *"This must be so."*

Yet Hamlet refuses to be consoled by this appeal to the generality of how things are and must be, and we believe he is right in his refusal, as Job is right in refusing the counsel of his friends. In the case of Hamlet's murdered father and the suffering of innocent Job, a specific injustice is involved. Bildad, Zophar, Gertrude, and Claudius all try to change the subject to the way things are. Perhaps so, answer the dying and the bereaved, but I know the way things are through the way things are with me. Extend the indictment, if you wish, to the way things are, but it is *this* case that I want to argue. Why her? Why him? Why me? Call it a logical fallacy, if you wish; it is this particular through which I implicate the whole. It is not life in general, but the particularity of *this* life lost that protests the edict that all must die.

A living organism, a biologist friend tells me, can be defined quite simply: It is something that can die. Where there is not death, there is not life. Such is the generality, and it would seem to be irrefutable. But that is very different from speaking of death in the first-person singular and, if we are capable of taking the risks of love, in the first-person plural.

In Tolstoy's *The Death of Ivan Ilyich*, the dying man suddenly recalls the textbook logic he learned so many years before. Caius is a man, all men are mortal, therefore Caius is mortal. "The example had seemed to him correct only in relation to Caius. Caius is in fact mortal and it is all very well for him to die; but for me the matter is entirely different."

Toward the very end, Ivan Ilyich, so pitiably turned in upon himself and his career, is moved, however hesitantly, to the first-person singular, and then to the plural. He receives Communion from the priest mainly to please his wife. The pain and the dying had been going on for weeks as he lay there on the sofa. "Then he felt that someone was kissing his hand. He opened his eyes, looked at his son, and felt sorry for him. His wife came up to him and he glanced at her. She was gazing at him open-mouthed, with undried tears on her nose and cheek and a despairing look on her face. He felt sorry for her too."

"Yes, I am making them wretched," he thought. "They are sorry, but it will be better for them when I die." He wished to say this but had not the strength to utter it. "Besides, why speak? I must act," he thought. With a look at his wife he indicated his son and said: "Take him away . . . sorry for him . . . sorry for you too . . ." He tried to add, "Forgive me," but said "Forego" and waved his hand, knowing that He whose understanding mattered would understand.

He looked for the pain that had been lashing him all these weeks. Ah, yes, there it was. "Well, what of it? Let the pain be."

He sought his former accustomed fear of death and did not find it. "Where is it? What death?" There was no fear because there was no death.

In place of death there was light.

"So that's what it is!" he suddenly exclaimed aloud. "What joy!"

To him all this happened in a single instant, and the meaning of that instant did not change. For those present his agony continued for another two hours. Something rattled in his throat, his emaciated body twitched, then the gasping and rattle became less and less frequent.

"It is finished!" said someone near him.

He heard these words and repeated them in his soul.

"Death is finished," he said to himself. "It is no more!"

He drew in a breath, stopped in the midst of a sigh, stretched out, and died.

The words, of course, are from the book of Revelation, chapter 21: "And I heard a voice from the throne saying, 'Behold, the dwelling of God is with men. He will dwell with them, and they shall be his people, and God himself will be with them; he will wipe away every tear from their eyes, and death shall be no more, neither shall there be mourning nor crying nor pain any more, for the former things have passed away.'" But for now we live, and die, among the former things.

Some leap forward in faith to what is to be, but for others that leap seems impossible. Perhaps for all of us, as for Ivan Ilyich, it will be only in that final "single instant" that we will *know* that death is no more. But then, it might be objected, we will be dead.

As I lay dying, death was ever present. The horizon was very much there, and drawing ever closer. I could not say, except in hope's anticipation, that death is no more. The rule that all that lives must die was holding true for me.

Two

SUCH IS THE GENERALITY, the warp and woof of everyday existence, with which the wise would learn to live. Through literature and imagination we would familiarize ourselves with death in the particular, knowing, or telling ourselves that we know, that it will one day force its familiarity upon us. And we tell ourselves that we are prepared. But then our wisdom is shattered, not by a sudden awareness of the generality, but by the singularity of a death—by the death of someone we love with a love inseparable from life. Or it is shattered by the imminent prospect of our own dying. With the cultivated complacency of the mass murderer that he was, Josef Stalin observed, "One death is a tragedy; a million deaths is a statistic." The newspapers report that another million have died in the ethnic slaughters in central Africa, while two million Christians and animists in Sudan have been killed by the radical Islamist regime in Khartoum. It is a great pity. How many are today dying at abortionists' hands? But as Dostoyevsky's Raskolnikov says, "Man gets used to everything—the beast."

Death in the thousands and millions is different. The generality is a buffer against both guilt and sorrow. It is death in the singular that shatters all we thought we knew about death. It is death in the singular that turns the problem of death into the catastrophe of death. Thus the lamentation of the philosopher Dietrich von Hildebrand: "I am filled with disgust and emptiness over the rhythm of everyday life that goes relentlessly on—as though nothing had changed, as though I had not lost my precious beloved!"

It used to be said that the Victorians of the nineteenth century talked incessantly about death but were silent about sex, whereas today we talk incessantly about sex and are silent about death. There is a measure of truth in that generalization, but only a measure. In 1973, Ernest Becker's *The Denial of Death* contended that Freud had gotten it exactly backwards. It is not true, said Becker, that our fear of death is rooted in our denial of sex, but, rather, that our fear of sex is rooted in our denial of death. Throughout history and in many cultures, sex and death have been engaged in a *danse macabre,* and not simply at the shadowed margins of erotic fantasy where dwell the likes of the Marquis de Sade, although that dance at the margins continues as well. In our day, the influential French intellectual Michel Foucault fascinated many with his sadomasochistic "limit experiences" in the bathhouses of San Francisco, until he died of AIDS. Here were death and sex marshaled against the supposed monotony of life. Death is invoked for the intensification of life.

Recall Walter Pater's counsel: "To burn always with this hard, gem-like flame, to maintain this ecstasy, is success in life." He goes on to say, "Failure is to form habits; for habit is relative to a stereotyped world." Only the experience matters, and experience is beyond convention or morality:

> The theory, or idea, or system, which requires of us the sacrifice of any part of this experience, in consideration of some interest into which we cannot enter, or some abstract morality we have not identified with ourselves, or what is only conventional, has no real claim upon us. . . . Not the fruit of experience, but experience itself is the end. . . . With this sense of the splendour of our experi-

ence and of its awful brevity, gathering all we are into one desperate effort to see and touch, we shall hardly have time to make theories about the things we see and touch.

Pater's is the creed of the complete aesthete: "For art comes to you professing frankly to give nothing but the highest quality to your moments as they pass, and simply for those moments' sake."

The intensity of life is increased by the awareness of its "awful brevity," and nowhere, Foucault and others have taken this to mean, is the "hard, gem-like flame" harder than at the edge of its extinction. The positive is accented, even revealed, by the negative. It is not only at the boundaries of life and death, of ecstasy and extinction, that this way of thinking plays itself out.

Consider the more everyday assumption that unhappiness is more interesting than happiness. Tolstoy's maxim in *Anna Karenina* is regularly cited: "Happy families are all alike; every unhappy family is unhappy in its own way." But is that really true? I have found just the opposite to be the case. An encounter with a happy family or happy marriage—where people love and support one another, where they find joy in the very being of the other—is almost always more fascinating than unhappiness. Unhappiness is a dreary replaying of deadly sins—envy, pride, resentment, hatred, and endless variations on the "old dreadfuls" of human depravity. It is all so very predictable. Happiness, by way of sharpest contrast, surprises and delights.

That troubling mystic Simone Weil wrote in *Gravity and Grace:* "We experience good only by doing it. We experience evil only by refusing to allow ourselves to do it, or, if we did it, by repenting of it." As with so many of her gnomic sayings, I am not entirely sure what she meant by that. But I think it means that the aesthete's and decadent's life "beyond good and evil" is, in fact, a delusion; it is the embrace of evil as good. We experience good by doing good, but we do not experience evil by doing evil, for in doing evil we make evil our good. The result is not life "beyond good and evil"; the result is the triumph of evil—a triumph more total because evil is not recognized as such. Evil, as Weil observed, is only experienced as evil in our refusing to do it, or, if we did it, by repenting of it. The terrors and excitements of sexuality and death are "limit conditions" of human existence. They represent life at the edge, and it should not surprise when those who are intolerant of limits join sex to death and death to sex in a desperate defiance they proclaim to be freedom.

These strange entanglements are not only played out at the margins, however. In sex and death are joined beginning and ending, the generative and the destructive. In contrast to a time not so far past when it was said that everybody talks about sex but nobody talks about death, in today's culture it is more true to say that we chatter incessantly about both sex and death. They are subjected to the specialization of experts, of therapists, ethicists, and the like. Sex and death have been "problematized," and problems are to be "solved" by sexual technique and the technology of dying. Victorian reticence about sex and our former reticence about death may have mystified both, although the probable intent was simply to put them out of mind. In any event, we have now embarked with a vengeance upon a course of demystification. Now there is nothing we cannot talk about in polite company. It is a great liberation. And a great loss, if in fact both sex and death partake of mystery. Mystery is attended by a fitting reticence.

That reticence is today violated in unprecedented ways, by, for instance, television documentaries that surround the dying and their families with microphones, cameras, lights, and the expert direction of show business. Such programs are typically in the service of "death with dignity," conveying a none too subtle advocacy of euthanasia and doctor-assisted suicide. But, of course, death with dignity is a delusion. Death is always the final indignity. Helplessness, loss of control, complete dependence on others, and imminent devastation can be borne with a measure of grace within a sacred space shared by those with whom the life now coming to an end was most importantly lived. To admit the public into what is finally entertainment aimed at ratings and market share is to violate the integrity of that ending. The dying gaze not into the eyes of those who have, with love, concern, and pleasure, watched over the years toward journey's end, but into a camera, and therefore into the eyes of a million strangers with remote control in hand, ready to switch channels the moment the drama begins to drag. Death is a private thing. It cannot be shared, it should not be shared, with those who did not know the inner rooms of the life whose doors are now closing.

"Should we ask the doctor to pull the plug?" The family huddles in televised consultation outside the room of the dying. This is cinema verité, and it is, after all, "educational" television. But it is not the cinema of truth about what people do and say when they are not on television. For those embroiled in the web of memories, resentments, and loves that surrounds the life now ending, a web of intimacies that nobody else can know, it is a violation of the mystery. We must not judge too harshly. Yes, some may take part in such travesties for the publicity, claiming the fifteen minutes of attention that Andy Warhol said is our due. But they tell themselves that they are doing it as a service, to help others who will one day have to go through the same thing. It is not the same thing. It is not the same thing at all when you are alone dying or with another who is dying, and all around you an indifferent world goes on with its business, as though this never-to-be-again moment is not happening.

The happening protected by reticence is not retrievable. You cannot later watch the broadcast of the last conversation with a close relative to see how you did. I know a family who videotaped their last moments with their dying mother, and what they videotaped was the family being videotaped. I am told there are couples who videotape themselves engaged in sexual intercourse, to be replayed later when erotic stimulus is desired. There is also a pornography of death, as Michel Foucault understood and perversely celebrated. Reticence is required to protect the mystery of sex and death. The two are linked in ways that escape the superficial. In the story of the Garden of Eden, our first parents recognized at the same time their nakedness and their mortality.

If we think about it, and even if we don't, sexual desire is directed beyond itself. It is as true for people as it is for animals. The salmon swim upstream to spawn, and then to die. That is the universal story. Animals enact it blindly; human beings can try to understand it. We intuit the bitter link between sex and death, a bitterness assuaged in part by procreation. In the sexual act our embarrassed neediness is on display. Nakedness represents defenselessness, and naked sex at its most aggressive is but aggression pitiably trying to disguise its dependence upon the response of the other. The hoped-for ecstasy of sexual union is a driving toward immortality, which is why the poetry of romantic love speaks incessantly of "forever." But we know it is not forever. In facing both sex and death, we can strive for a balance between reticence and candor, but such a balance is elusive, for it is in the nature of both to throw us off balance.

Surely it is a good thing that we are, for the most part, beyond the time when the family engaged in a conspiracy of silence and lies to prevent Aunt Hannah from knowing the doctors said that there is nothing more to be done, that she is dying. Thus did well-meaning families and friends once deprive those they loved of the opportunity to prepare for death. If, that is, the conspiracy was successful, which I expect it was not most of the time. Remember Burl Ives as Big Daddy in the film *Cat on a Hot Tin Roof*? He knows he is dying of cancer, his family knows he is dying of cancer, and yet they assure him that he will soon be well. "Mendacity! Mendacity! I'm surrounded by mendacity!" he rages in anguish and anger. It is wrong to tell lies. It is terribly wrong to surround with mendacity the moment of life that ought to be an uncompromised moment of truth—a moment that, faced honestly or dishonestly evaded, will come for all of us.

Reticence is not a refusal to talk about what is happening, and it is certainly not a denial of what is happening. Reticence means reserve, restraint, and a respect that verges on reverence. This life is now coming to an end; *this* life, a life never lived before and never to be lived again. This person lying there on the bed so hopelessly helpless, who, it seems not all that long ago, was held in her mother's arms so hopefully helpless; who was dandled on her uncle's lap as the family happily remarked on her resemblance to her grandmother; who was terrified of her first day of school, exultant when asked to the prom, so proud of her first job, so grateful when her son Jimmy recovered after the doctors said he had a month at most, and so handsomely matriarchal in the light blue dress that was remade for the fortieth wedding anniversary.

It is *this* life never lived before and never to be lived again that is now coming to an end. It is a time for reticence. A time for "Remember when?" in the intimate circle of those who shared this life. Remember when with tears, remember when with laughter. And, when memory has failed the one who is dying, it is a time for those who can remember to remind, in the hope that behind the fog of forgetfulness is, somewhere, a capacity to recall that has only lost its voice. Above all, it is a matter of being there, of offering to the helpless the last gift that is our helplessness—with the hope, please God, that a lifetime of confused reachings toward immortality will yet be vindicated.

This is the brute fact, however: There is an ending, and the sadness of it dare not be denied. When I was in the intensive-care unit, wired to so many bleeping and ticking machines that my body seemed at times to be part of the machinery, the words of Psalm 103 pressed upon my mind:

> *As for man, his days are like grass;*
> *he flourishes like a flower of the field;*
> *for the wind passes over it, and it is gone,*
> *and its place knows it no more.*

"And its place knows it no more." Our lives are like a blade of grass in a vast field of billions of blades of grass. Or I may think my life to be a flower, unique in its beauty. No matter, it is soon gone, and even the minuscule piece of earth that it occupied knows it no more. The bitterness is assuaged in part, but only in part, if in our lives we brought new life into being. People may think that they live on in the chromosomes and genes they impart to their children, but it takes only a little arithmetic to know that what we impart is halved, and with each generation halved again and again, until what is left is even more minuscule than the place that knows the blade of grass no more. Moreover, the life of a child, and even more of a child's child, is, as it is actually lived, formed by others—and by terrors, hopes, and dreams—serenely indifferent to who *we* were. To those who come after us and to those who come after them, we are the past, the ever more distant past. They may try to remember fondly, but, in truth, they know us no more.

"Life must go on," we say, and we know as we say it that we are also saying that lives must end. In sexual intercourse, human beings defiantly wave a little flag in the face of mortality and, in the excitement of the moment, can forget the futility of the gesture. Upon reflection, we understand that we have only played our little part in the relentless succession of blades and flowers whose places know them no more. And yet, and yet. . . . It is no little thing to have played one's part. And there is the irrepressible intuition that maybe, just maybe, it is part of a greater whole in which each little place remembers who once was there. That maybe, just maybe, the "forever" in the speaking of our love is not a delusion.

Van Gogh's paintings contain symbolism that was largely free of the theorizing of his time and of every time. Of his *Wheatfield with Reaper*, he wrote to his brother: "I saw in this reaper the image of death, in the sense that humanity could be the wheat being reaped. But in that death, there is nothing sad, it occurs in bright light with a sun drenching everything with a light of spun gold. It is an image of death such as the great book of nature tells us about—but what I sought was the almost, smiling." The appeal to the course of nature, of accepting what cannot be helped, is a Stoic note. But what he more deeply sought drew, I believe, upon Christian hope. He sought the almost, smiling.

"And its place knows it no more." I think of all the places I have known and that I like to think, perhaps irrationally, have known me. Creatures of time and space that we are, the spaces of our lives are as much a part of who we are as the times of our lives. It is an old Russian custom for one going on a journey to sit quietly for at least five minutes, saying good-bye to the

space one is leaving. To this living room, this bedroom, this kitchen, "Good-bye, dear room. Remember
what we did together here, how we loved and laughed
and cried. Remember me, as I will remember you." I
confess that over the years, on the lecture circuit and
attending conferences, I have paused to bid good-bye
to innumerable rooms in hotels and motels. If only for
one night, a nondescript, anonymous space shared my
life, and, if space has a history, I was part of its life. In
the days and months that followed, others would share
that space, would sleep on that hotel bed—exhausted
sales representatives, grandparents on their way to
visit a sick child, perhaps prostitutes. We will never
know one another, but we have in common that we
once shared this space; this space has us in common.
Years ago one commonly saw, and still sees occasionally today, the graffito "Kilroy was here." We want
the times and spaces of our lives to remember us. But
the psalm is relentless: "And its place knows it no more."

Then there are the spaces we truly cherished, that
are inseparable from who we once were and will always be. The attic bedroom in Pembroke, Ontario—
357 Miller Street, to be exact—where the rain rico-
cheted off the tin roof, and I could see from the bed
my empire of toy trains extending across the entire
floor. Six engines, switches galore, and passenger cars

with leather seats and little interior lights—the gift of an uncle who, he said, looted it from a castle of Hermann Göring during the occupation of Germany. That attic bedroom was the space of magic. When I was eight or nine years old, I painted an arrow on the wall of the landing that went up to the attic with the words "To Dick Neuhaus's Abode." (I thought "abode" a very fancy word.) The sign was still there several years ago, when last I visited the house—only to discover, of course, that the house had shrunk to about half the size it was when I was a child. Maybe by now somebody has painted over the sign. Inevitably, somebody soon will. Is it possible that my attic could forget me? I have not forgotten it, and never will. That is where I read *Black Beauty* and *Ben Hur* and Captain Marvel comics without end. That is where I dreamed about going off to school, about doing important things in a world bigger than my attic could imagine. One day, I thought, I will come back to my attic bedroom and tell the rafters and the windows and the big chimney in the middle of the floor all that has happened to me. But when last I visited, the attic was being used for storage and was filled with boxes and crates and files. My place knew me no more.

Life goes on. In even the most hospitable times and spaces, we are guests but for a time. Time and space are embarrassed by our attempting to return. We are soon the past, and things have moved on. "Adjusting to the Light" is Miller Williams's reflection on the embarrassment of friends and neighbors when Lazarus returns from the dead. He was gone only four days, but already it is not easy to fit him back into things.

> Lazarus, listen, we have things to tell you.
> We killed the sheep you meant to take to market.
> We couldn't keep the old dog, either.
> He minded you. The rest of us he barked at.
> Rebecca, who cried two days, has given her hand
> to the sandalmaker's son. Please understand
> we didn't know that Jesus could do this.
>
> We're glad you're back. But give us time to think.
> Imagine our surprise . . . We want to say
> we're sorry for all that. And one thing more.
> We threw away the lyre. But listen, we'll pay
> whatever the sheep was worth. The dog, too.
> And put your room the way it was before.

Four days is not a long time. The time will come, in fact already is, when things cannot be put back the way they were before. Of this blade of grass, of this life, it will be said, "Its place knows it no more." At the family cottage on the Ottawa River, my five-year-old godson, Stephen Paul, says on our last day, "Good-bye, Mister Sun!" as, in a blaze of vermilion splendor, it slips beneath the horizon. Then, wrinkling his little brow, he looks up and asks me, "Will he know us when we come back next year?" I say that I hope so, knowing that soon I will be gone, soon his parents will be gone, and, if he and his sisters still visit the cottage, soon they will be gone, and Mister Sun will in indifferent splendor go on doing what he has done for millions of years. It seems unfair that the times and places to which we have given so much of ourselves should know us no more. Our little story is one of unrequited love for a world that moves on.

Most unfair, however, is that the people whom we loved should know us no more. Not only in making love, as it is said, and in marriage, but in every true friendship there is an element of the erotic. In the perfect harmony of souls, eros holds out the promise of time standing still. It is an unfortunate person who has never known a moment of communion with another that is unsurpassable, and therefore, were there justice in the world, should never pass. That the sublime and the perverse should join in the erotic defiance of death is no surprise. The connections between sex and mortality are not evident to everyone. Among the healthy-minded graduates of what is called sex education, sex is an appetite to be satisfied or good clean sport. Appetite and play enter into sex, of course, or else there would be little sex and even fewer babies. We can refuse to think or, having thought, can willfully blind ourselves to so much else that is engaged: to sex as the enactment of love, which is the gift of self, which is the loss of self. A newspaper advertisement for a geriatric remedy pictures a couple in their sixties and urges the reader to "rediscover the sex of your teenage years." The aged in their rheumatoid writhings can for a moment, and for a price, forget that they are going to die, that they are dying. On offer is regression to a time when "forever" had not been put to the test of life's disappointed forevers.

With the end of reticence and the "demystification" of the depth dimension of human existence, it is perhaps not surprising that death and dying has become a popular topic of everyday chatter. "Support groups" for the bereaved crop up all over. How to "cope" with dying is a regular subject on television talk shows. It no doubt has something to do with the growing number of old people in the population. "So many more people seem to die these days," remarked my elderly aunt as she looked over the obituary columns in the local daily. Obituaries routinely include medical details once thought to be the private business of the family. Every evening without fail, at least in our cities, the television news carries a "sob shot" of relatives who have lost someone in an accident or crime. "And how did you feel when you saw she was dead?" The intrusiveness is shameless, and taboos once broken are hard to put back together again. But we can try. Maybe we can't do it for the whole culture; but for ourselves and for those we love, we can try.

THREE

EVELYN WAUGH'S *The Loved One* brilliantly satirized and Jessica Mitford's *The American Way of Death* brutally savaged the death industry of commercial exploitation. Years later it may be time for a similarly critical look at the psychology-of-death industry that got under way in 1969 when Elisabeth Kübler-Ross set forth her five stages of grieving—denial, anger, bargaining, depression, and acceptance. No doubt many people feel they have been helped by formal and informal therapies for bereavement and, if they feel they have been helped, they probably have been in some way that is not unimportant. Just being able to get through the day without cracking up is no little thing. But neither, one may suggest, is it the most important thing. I have listened to people who speak with studied, almost clinical, detail about where they are in their trek through the five stages. Death and bereavement are "processed." There are hundreds of self-help books on how to cope with death in order to get on with life. This little book is not of that genre.

A measure of reticence and silence is in order. There is a time simply to be present to death—whether one's own or that of others—without any felt urgencies to do something about it or get over it. The Preacher had it right: "For everything there is a season, and a time for every matter under heaven: a time to be born, and a time to die;. . . a time to mourn, and a time to dance." The time of mourning should be given its due. One may be permitted to wonder about the wisdom of contemporary funeral rites that hurry to the dancing, displacing sorrow with the determined affirmation of resurrection hope, supplying a ready answer to a question that has not been given time to understand itself. One may even long for something so countercultural as the Dies Irae, the sequence at the old Requiem Mass:

> *Dies irae, dies illa,*
> *solvet saeclum in favilla,*
> *teste David cum Sibylla.*

> The day of wrath, that day
> will consume the world in ashes,
> as David and the Sibyl prophesied.

Mors stupebit et natura.
Cum resurget creatura
judicanti responsura.

> Death and nature will stand amazed
> when creation rises again
> to answer to the Judge.

Recordare, Jesu pie,
quod sum causa tuae viae
ne me perdas illa die.

> Recall, merciful Jesus,
> that I am the reason for thy earthly
> journey;
> do not destroy me on that day.

Qui Mariam absolvisti
et latronem exaudisti,
mihi quoque spem dedisti.

> Thou who didst absolve Mary
> [Magdalen]
> and didst hear the prayer of the thief
> hast given me hope, too.

Ora supplex et acclinis
cor contritum quasi cinis,
gere curam mei finis.

> I pray, kneeling in supplication,
> my heart as contrite as ashes:
> take Thou mine ending into Thy care.

Huic ergo parce, Deus,
pie Jesu Domine:
dona eis requiem. Amen.

> Therefore spare this one, O God,
> merciful Lord Jesus;
> grant them rest. Amen.

Life is taken seriously when life is held to account, our lives and the lives of others. The worst thing is not the sorrow or the loss or the heartbreak. It is to be encountered by death and not to be changed by the encounter. There are pills we can take to get through the experience, but the danger is that we then do not go through the experience but around it. At this point one must speak with care. In the last thirty years, we have become accustomed to the fact that a large part of the population, from those in grade school through those in nursing homes, is more or less permanently on mind-altering, mood-altering drugs. No doubt such pharmacological relief makes many people feel better, and makes schoolboys and inmates more manageable. It seems merciless to argue with those whose medication provides respite from the deep melancholy we now call clinical depression. And yet, I believe we should not get used to the ease with which we resort to chemical relief, to the dulling of the sharp edges of experience.

In the seventeenth century, Robert Burton wrote *Anatomy of Melancholy*, a brilliant examination of human sensibilities lifted to exultant heights and cast into the abyss of despair. Falling in love, love unrequited, loss of the beloved, fear of damnation, and the meaninglessness of existence—all are explored with wit, learning, and relentless honesty. All are part, Burton suggests, of the fullness of the human experience. "The Tower of Babel," Burton writes, "never yielded such confusion of tongues as this Chaos of Melancholy doth variety of symptoms." He goes on to issue the warning, "I would advise him, that is actually melancholy, not to read this Tract of Symptomes, lest he disquiet or make himselfe for a time worse, and more melancholy than he was before." A century later the great Samuel Johnson, who today would almost certainly be diagnosed as clinically depressed for long periods of his life, praised the *Anatomy* highly. In *Vanity of Human Wishes*, Dr. Johnson asks, "Must helpless man, in ignorance sedate, / Roll darkling down the torrent of his fate?" Today that "sedate" takes on a somewhat different meaning. The sedated ignorance of Eliot's chorus in *Murder in the Cathedral* who are "living, living, and partly living" may be the price to be paid for prizing happiness, understood as a sense of well-being, as our highest good. In our mourning for another, drugs may sometimes have their uses in confronting death, but to be sedated against death is to join the pitiable chorus of the living, living, and partly living.

In her engaging and instructive anthology *The Nature of Melancholy*, Jennifer Radden notes that the term *melancholy* comes from two Greek words, *melas* ("black") and *khole* ("bile"). Melancholy has to do with humoral states, the ancient Greeks taught. As there are four elements—earth, air, fire, and water—so human health depends upon the right balance among four humors, or substances, in the body: blood, phlegm, black bile, and yellow bile. The spleen was commonly thought to be the villain in producing black bile, an excessive amount of which produced melancholy, although sometimes blame was attached to the gallbladder as well. During my emergency surgeries, the spleen was removed, and, some years later, my gallbladder. I do not know what that means for my vulnerability to melancholy.

Radden suggests that in the Age of Prozac, as our time has been called, scientific thinking about melancholy, or depression, has come full circle back to the theory of the humors. Other theories were fashionable for a time. Immanuel Kant proposed that melancholy, indeed all mental disorder, has its cause in illogical, false beliefs, or delusion. Get your ideas in order and all will be well. Almost nobody today is a Kantian on that score. Freud, as one might expect, had fascinating, if fantastical, theories about loss, narcissistic retrojection, and longing for the mother's breast as the cause of melancholy. In the late twentieth century, some feminist theorists contended that melancholy, especially melancholy in women, was culturally constructed by a gender-twisting patriarchal society. But after all these centuries, the dominant scientific view today is that of the science of Greek antiquity: melancholy is caused by an imbalance of things, call them humors, in the body. The big difference today, of course, is that relentless experimentation has discovered that drugs can somehow or other—nobody knows quite how or why—affect such imbalances and relieve the symptoms of melancholy, now called depression.

Aristotle, Hippocrates, Galen, and other worthies understood that the human being is both body and soul—an embodied soul or, as some preferred, an ensouled body. The body affects the soul, and the soul affects the body. The effect of the body on the soul depends on what, for lack of a better term, they called the humors. It is not evident that we have a better term today. What we do have is much greater experimental knowledge about the pharmaceutical manipulation of whatever-they-are-to-be-called. That is, for many people, a great blessing—unless the power to manipulate seduces them into believing, along with the materialists of yesterday and today, that they do not have a soul.

The unhappy truth is that some are seduced into believing that. First published in 1932, Aldous Huxley's *Brave New World* becomes more timely with every passing year. In the brave new world where babies are made to order and all is expertly managed to assure contentment and preclude questions or anxieties, there is no place for life's intensities, whether of good or evil. And where the order is not yet perfected and intensity threatens, there is always *soma*, the pharmacological return to the safety of comfortable equilibrium. To a character in the story who does not understand, it is explained:

"And there's always *soma* to calm your anger, to reconcile you to your enemies, to make you patient and long-suffering. In the past you could only accomplish these things by making a great effort and after years of hard moral training. Now you swallow two or three half-gramme tablets, and there you are. Anybody can be virtuous now.

You can carry at least half your morality about in a bottle. Christianity without tears—that's what *soma* is."

A young writer not sufficiently conditioned to the brave new world submits for publication a paper titled "A New Theory of Biology." The Controller, who is old enough to remember the former order, rules that it must not be published, but he does so with a touch of regret. "It was a masterly piece of work. But once you began admitting explanations in terms of purpose—well, you didn't know what the result might be." People may "lose their faith in happiness as the Sovereign Good and take to believing, instead, that the goal was somewhere beyond, somewhere outside the present human sphere; that the purpose of life was not the maintenance of well-being but some intensification and refining of consciousness, some enlargement of knowledge." All that may be true, he regretfully thinks, but it is not admissible in the brave new world. "What fun it would be," he thinks, "if one didn't have to think about happiness!" When happiness is dethroned as the Sovereign Good, it is not always fun, of course. But the result is intensification, it is time as drama, it is life lived against the horizon of death.

Traditions of wisdom encourage us not to draw back from intensification; more specifically, they encourage us to stay with death a while. Among observant Jews, those closest to the deceased observe shiva for seven days following the death. During shiva one does not work, bathe, put on shoes, engage in intercourse, read Torah, or have his hair cut. The mourners are to behave as though they themselves have died. The first response to death is to give inconsolable grief its due. Such grief is assimilated during the seven days of shiva and then tempered by a month of more moderate mourning. After a year all mourning is set aside, except for the praying of kaddish, the prayer for the dead, on the anniversary of the death.

It does not happen in clinical stages, but in staying with unspeakable loss the intensifications are modulated through time. *A Grief Unveiled* is Gregory Floyd's account of losing a five-year-old son, John-Paul, who was run over and killed by a passing car. Floyd writes, "There is a difference between early grief and later grief. Early grief is acute; later grief is more diffuse. Early grief smacks, stings, punches; later grief is more gentle. Early grief is a stalker; later grief is a companion. Early grief is crags and crevices; later grief is furrows softened by the passage of time."

In *The Blood of the Lamb*, Peter de Vries, who lost a young daughter to leukemia, calls us to "the recognition of how long, how very long, is the mourners' bench upon which we sit, arms linked in undeluded friendship—all of us, brief links ourselves, in the eternal pity." From the pity we may hope that wisdom has been distilled, a wisdom from which we can benefit when we take the place that is reserved for us on the mourners' bench. Philosophy means the love of wisdom, and so some may look to philosophers in their time of loss and aloneness. George Santayana wrote, "A good way of testing the caliber of a philosophy is to ask what it thinks of death." What does it tell us that modern philosophy has had relatively little to say about death? Ludwig Wittgenstein wrote, "What can be said at all can be said clearly; and whereof one cannot speak thereof one must be silent." There is undoubtedly wisdom in such reticence, which stands in refreshing contrast to the endless therapeutic chatter of popular culture. But those who sit, arms linked in undeluded friendship, cannot help but ask and wonder.

At age nineteen, without any warning, Augustine's most beloved friend died. He writes in the *Confessions* that he was appalled at a world that could go on as though this catastrophe had not happened. Death had thrown the world and his part in the world into question. *Factus eram ipse mihi magna quaestio*—"I had become a great question to myself." It has been said with some justice that that sentence marks the beginning of existentialist philosophy. Not, of course, in Augustine's case, the agnostic or atheistic existentialism of self-dramatizing individualism that was such a fashion in the twentieth century. Rather, through the experience of his friend's death was born the awareness that nothing can be taken for granted, that existence itself is a question calling for an answer. And with that, the awareness of wonder.

One might think that death would not come to a Christian as a surprise. St. Paul writes in chapter 6 of his letter to the Romans, "Do you not know that all of us who have been baptized into Christ Jesus were baptized into his death? We were buried therefore with him by baptism into death, so that as Christ was raised from the dead by the glory of the Father, we too might walk in newness of life." During those long nights, or days that seemed as night, in the intensive-care unit, the dominating thought was that I almost died, and am dying. And then this: That I am only now completing my baptism, a baptism that happened many years ago when I was two weeks old.

It is Christian teaching that the *sacrament* of Baptism is completed by the *sacrament* of Confirmation, when the child is old enough to freely appropriate the grace already given. But I learned that there is a further rite of confirmation in dying; in death is abandonment in the company of the One who on the cross was abandoned. Here is born a wonder more intense than any wonder ever wondered before. "Ah, so this is how it is!" And with that an intimation, but only an intimation, of the possibility, but only the possibility, of newness of life. I am, however, getting ahead of my story.

Return to philosophy, where the world is a question and we are a question to ourselves. All philosophy begins in wonder, said the ancients. With exceptions, contemporary philosophy stops at wonder. We are told: Don't ask, don't wonder about what you cannot know for sure. Accept nothing as true, said Descartes, that you can reasonably doubt. With that, I am convinced, the world called modern took a fateful wrong turn. The most important things about life and everyday living we cannot know for sure. We cannot know them beyond all possibility of their turning out to be false. We order our loves and loyalties, we invest our years with meaning and our death with hope, not knowing for sure, beyond all reasonable doubt, whether we might not have gotten it wrong. What we need is a philosophy that enables us to speak truly, if not clearly, a wisdom that does not eliminate but comprehends our doubt.

A long time ago, when I was a young pastor in a very black and very poor inner-city parish that could not pay a salary, I worked part-time as chaplain at Kings County Hospital in Brooklyn. With more than three thousand beds, Kings County boasted then of being the largest medical center in the world. It seems primitive now, but back then not much of a fuss was made about those who were beyond reasonable hope of recovery. They were almost all poor people, and this was before Medicare or Medicaid, so it was, as we used to say, a charity hospital. They were sedated, and food was brought for those who could eat. The dying, male and female, had their beds lined up side by side in a huge ward, fifty to a hundred of them at any given time. On hot summer days and without air-conditioning, they would fitfully toss off sheets and undergarments. The scene of naked and half-naked bodies groaning and writhing was reminiscent of Dante's *Inferno*.

Hardly a twenty-four-hour stint would go by without my accompanying two or three or more people to their death. One such death is indelibly imprinted upon my memory. His name was Albert, a man of about seventy and (I don't know why it sticks in my mind) completely bald. That hot summer morning I had prayed with him and read the Twenty-third Psalm. Toward evening, I went up again to the death ward— for so everybody called it—to see him again. Clearly the end was near. Although he had been given a sedative, he was entirely lucid. I put my left arm around his shoulder and together, face almost touching face, we prayed the Our Father. Then Albert's eyes opened wider, as though he had seen something in my expression. "Oh," he said, "oh, don't be afraid." His body sagged back and he was dead. Stunned, I realized that, while I thought I was ministering to him, his last moment of life was expended in ministering to me.

There is also another death that will not leave me. Charlie Williams was a deacon of St. John the Evangelist in Brooklyn. (We sometimes called the parish St. John the Mundane in order to distinguish it from St. John the Divine, the Episcopal cathedral up in Morningside Heights.) Charlie was an ever ebullient and sustaining presence through rough times. In the face of every difficulty, he had no doubt that "Jesus is going to see us through." Then something went bad in his chest, and the doctors made medically erudite noises to cover their ignorance. I held his hand as he died a painful death at age forty-three. Through the blood that bubbled up from his hemorrhaging lungs he formed his last word. Very quietly, not complaining but deeply puzzled, he looked up at me and asked, "Why?"

Between Albert's calm assurance and Charlie's puzzlement, who is to say which is the Christian way to die? I have been with some who screamed defiance, others who screamed with pain, and many who just went to sleep. Typically today the patient is heavily sedated and plugged into sundry machines. One only knows that death has come when the bleeping lines on the monitors go flat or the attending physician nods his head in acknowledgment of medicine's defeat. It used to be that we accompanied sisters and brothers to their final encounter. Now we mostly sit by and wait. The last moment that we are really with them, and they with us, is often hours or even many days before they die. But medical technology notwithstanding, for each one of them, for each one of us, at some point "it" happens.

Of some places and times, it is the smell we remember best. Kings County had a cavernous emergency ward, and on weekend nights it was bedlam with the victims of shootings, knifings, brawls, beatings, and accidents labeled "cause unknown." And everywhere one breathed the smell of blood.

In Stalin's prisons, where countless died, the Russian poet Anna Akhmatova said about that smell of blood:

> Wild honey smells like freedom,
> Dust—like a ray of sun.
> Like violets—a young maid's mouth,
> And gold—like nothing.
> The flowers of the mignonette smell like water,
> And like an apple—love.

But we learned once and for all
That blood smells only like blood.

Back at Kings County, near midnight on a sweaty August Saturday, they hustled her in from the ambulance: her dress soaked in blood still hot, the broken bone of her forearm sticking through her flesh, her face slashed, apparently by a broken bottle. Not a beer bottle, however, for it had shattered, and there were little pieces of clear glass, blood-marked glittering glass, stuck in her forehead, her cheeks, her chin. She was, I thought, bedecked for death as though with diamonds. Her eyelids flickered two or three times, she looked, as though recognizing someone or something, and then "it" happened. The few brief medical formalities, and the intern wrote on the chart "DOA"—dead on arrival—but in fact she had arrived to die. We didn't say a word, but I think we both understood that she was owed, and that is why slowly, almost ritually, we picked out the glittering shards of glass from her pretty black face. I put the diamonds in a small plastic bag and kept them for years, but I no longer know where they are. I remember the smell, though, the smell of blood, which smells only like blood.

She was among the thousands who are never claimed. I have wondered about the one who did it to her. Was she his wife, his lover, a pickup at a bar? Has he ever wondered what happened to her? Has he ever known remorse? Her unclaimed body, like so many others for almost two centuries now, was put in a numbered wooden box and trucked out to Potter's Field on Hart Island in the East River, a vast and desolate place barren of grass or flowers, only row upon row of plain little signs bearing numbers upon numbers. A large stone is erected in the midst of Potter's Field and on it are inscribed the words "He Knows Them by Name." He knows her by name.

When there is nothing more to be done, being there is all. The doctors told Gregory and Maureen that John-Paul was comatose, there was no brain activity, he would not return. At home, they gathered the other children, and Gregory explained, "Johnny is very sick and he is probably going to die." They began to cry. "It's okay to cry. You can cry as much as you like because it's a very sad time." They were going to go to the hospital together. "I want to tell you what Johnny is going to look like. He's lying on a bed. He's covered with a sheet, just like at home. He looks like he's asleep, and he has a lot of wires attached to him. The wires don't hurt him. They help the doctors and the nurses to know how he's doing and whether he needs anything." But now Johnny only needed, and they only needed, the being there.

Mother, father, and the five children gathered around the bed where they could see Johnny, touch him, and tell him whatever needed to be told. Only four-year-old Rose seemed not to understand what was happening. The nurses were crying, the priest was crying. One by one, the children touched his face, his arms, his legs.

"Johnny, you're such a good brother."

"Johnny, please don't die."

"I love you so much, Johnny."

Gregory told them it was their last family prayer time with Johnny. "Let's sing whatever he'd like to sing."

They sang "Shine, Jesus, Shine" and a few of his other favorites, and then little Gregory, the ten-year-old, said they should tell John-Paul that they were sorry for anything bad they ever said or did to him and ask his forgiveness, and when they had done that, they each walked to his head, whispered into his ear, and kissed him good-bye. Then the children went home, while Gregory and Maureen kept vigil until the official statement that "it" had happened.

Some may think the scene too consoling, even maudlin. But that happened. The death of adults who know they are dying is different. A noted medical authority who has written extensively on death and dying says that he doubts there is such a thing as a peaceful death, and never once in all his years, he says, has he witnessed a person finding final consolation in religious faith. I don't know what to tell him in response. Is it possible his patients view him as a medical technician and not a person in whom they could confide? A psychologist who works with the dying tells me that my experience reflects the fact that, because I am a priest, people feel obliged to put on a brave face in order to hide the terror they feel. There may be something to that. It seems more likely, however, that to a priest they vent their inmost thoughts, their rage at the wrongness of what is happening, their remorse over a life now ending that was not what they had hoped it would be and now it is too late. I expect the priest, or at least the attentive priest, sees more of the rawness of human desperation than do others who work with people who are at the edges of life. But I will not argue the point. Are we to get into statistics and the calibration of degrees of terror and tranquillity at the end? That strikes me as absurd, and a cruel violation of the unrepeatable particularity of persons facing, with whatever spiritual and moral resources are theirs, the end. I speak of my own times with the dying, of what I have learned from others who accompanied those whom they loved, and of what I learned as I lay dying.

Elizabeth—everybody called her Betsy—was eighty-three years old and the matriarch of an extended family. She was a handsome woman of great dignity and self-possession, but in the last years her mind wandered, which does not mean it was lost. She would come and go, as it were, to and from different countries, and it was by no means evident to me which was the shadowland and which what we call reality. She knew she was dying and, like so many, wondered why the Lord was taking so long. Hers had been, as they say, a rich life; rich in family, friendships, faith, and accomplishments. In the last weeks she repeated again and again one request, really a demand: "Tell Harold I'm sorry. Promise me you'll tell him." Harold was her husband, and he had died almost twenty years ago. Of course I promised, not knowing how I would keep the promise, or if I ever could, or which of us would see Harold first, if at all.

"I'm sorry." "Ask her (or him) to forgive me." "Will God forgive me?" Such are the commonplaces of the deathbed. Part remorse, part contrition, part complaint that time has run out and there is no opportunity to gather up the loose ends and put things in order—these are the repeated sentiments, even of those who say they are ready to die, indeed eager to die. Life is ended, but it is not finished, and now it is too late. And that is the way it is.

To be sure, others are anything but resigned. They protest that they have been cheated by time's running out. Querulous souls, they point out that this should have happened and that should have happened, and what if . . . and if only. . . . "What if" and "if only" loom large in such meanderings of discontent. Sarah at Kings County was like that in her restless ending, and years later she still comes to mind while reading the lines of e. e. cummings:

> *wherelings whenlings,*
> *(daughters of ifbut offsprings of*
> *hopefear*
> *sons of unless and children of almost)*
> *never shall guess the dimension of*
>
> *him whose*
> *each*
> *foot likes the*
> *here of this earth*
>
> *whose both*
> *eyes*
> *love*
> *this now of the sky*

Wherelings, whenlings, daughters of ifbut, and children of almost. Living always contingently, hoping for that thing that would make life begin, and then life is over and it never began. Kevin, as I shall call him, was for ten years part of the community where I live. In his late thirties, he was dying of AIDS. When as a very young man he arrived in New York to attend acting school (he was a Shakespearean actor of considerable talent), he was captivated by the city's underworld of erotic disorder. That was years ago, but he carried within him, for a long time unknowingly, the deadly sequel of those misspent days and nights. At community dinners I had told, undoubtedly more than once, a favorite story: Around 1910, William Temple, the future archbishop of Canterbury and son of Frederick, the archbishop of Canterbury, complained to his father that he did not have the time to do all that needed to be done. "William," said his father, "you have all the time there is." I tell myself that frequently, especially when I am worried about getting done more than it is mine to do: You have all the time there is.

Time is not unlike a sacrament; it is capable of bearing the absolute. Christian thinkers have written about the "sacramentality of the present moment." Our lives are lived in a succession of present moments, and the trick is to slow down the pace at which one moment is succeeded by another. "Be still, and know that I am God," says Psalm 46. But our world presents itself as a conspiracy against being still, against living in the present moment. I walk out on Second Avenue and the people, the cars, the trucks, the buses, the very buildings themselves, along with an impetuous drive within myself to be someplace I am not, are all pressing up against the enemy of the present moment that is The Future, which is to say the next present moment that is, in turn, to be escaped as rapidly as possible into the next present moment; like a rushing crowd trying to get out of a burning building through a tiny exit. Having never stopped to live the present moment, we one day run out of present moments and discover we have not lived at all. It is true in every present moment: You have all the time there is.

Kevin was terribly thin, and almost nothing in his enfeebled, drug-dosed body worked the way it should. He was quite blind by this point. It was shortly after my major surgeries. Sitting face to face in his apartment, for it had been a long time since he could get out, we were two sorry specimens: a young life blasted and another seemingly played out. The difference was that his doctors offered him no hope, while mine spoke of my getting better. That is a not unimportant difference; he was moving toward death and I away from death. But between us, or so I believe, there was no divide. We were in the same place. I told him what I thought I had learned while lying at death's door. He spoke to me calmly and—this is the wonder—gratefully of all the undeserved good he had known in his life. He paused only to adjust the tube taped to his left arm and to catch his breath with the help of the inhalator now always by his side. Then he smiled and looked at me with his unseeing eyes, actually looking about six inches to my right, for his hearing was off as well. He wanted me to know that he was not afraid. Nor was he bitter. He said that he had had all the time there is, and still did. It was one afternoon some weeks later that he said he was going to take a nap. He never woke up.

Kevin was not a whereling or whenling, a son of if-but or a child of almost. What was ended was finished. His foot liked the here of this earth, and his eyes, even those blind eyes, loved a now that never ends. A good death? you ask. Yes, I think so. An unspeakably messy death, and a long descent into the humiliation of helplessness, but a helplessness understood as dependence upon grace. His was a long deliberated dying.

Quite different is sudden death, especially of the young. We have those wrenching accounts of the trenches in World War I: at the Sommes and Ypres, hundreds of thousands scrambling through mud and splattered guts, hurled back by the mechanical relentlessness of machine-gun fire, screaming for their mothers. As a boy I was greatly moved by Rupert Brooke and others who poetically chronicled the senseless slaughter of the young. But even more was I moved by the familiar stories of the Christian martyrs of the Roman Empire, especially the young martyrs, who deliberated their dying and came as close as perhaps is humanly possible to choosing death for the sake of life.

There is another story told me when I was very young, by a veteran who said he was there. Allied troops were on a ship crossing the English Channel. For some reason I forget—perhaps it was torpedoed—the ship was sinking, and fifty or more men were caught in the hold, from which there was no escape. A chaplain who was on deck with the other soldiers went down through the one-way funnel to his certain death in order to give Last Rites or otherwise console those who were still alive. I have over the years been haunted by that story of what it means to be a minister, a servant, of the One who said, "I have come not to be served but to serve." The veteran who told it to me emphasized that none of the soldiers would have blamed the chaplain had he stayed on the safety of the deck, but neither did they try to dissuade him from his determination to temper fate with grace. I have thought about what I would have done were I in his place, and I do not know.

It has often been said that each death is unique, that each of us must die our own death. Enthusiasts such as

Walt Whitman gild the inevitable. "Nothing can happen more beautiful than death," he writes in *Leaves of Grass*. In "Song of Myself" he trumpets: "Has anyone supposed it lucky to be born? / I hasten to inform him or her, it is just as lucky to die, and I know it." Good for him. Willa Cather kept me company during the months of surgeries, chemotherapy, and endless tests. Of Walt Whitman she wrote:

He is sensual, not after the manner of Swinburne and Gautier, who are always seeking for perverted and bizarre effects on the senses, but in the frank fashion of the old barbarians who ate and slept and smacked their lips over the mead horn. He is rigidly limited to the physical, things that quicken his pulses, please his eyes or delight his nostrils. There is an element of poetry in all this, but it is by no means the highest. If a joyous elephant should break forth into song, his lay would probably be very much like Whitman's famous "Song of Myself." It would have just about as much delicacy and deftness and discrimination.

That seems to me about right. His trumpeting amounts to this: I am Walt Whitman. I am life itself. It follows that, if I die, it is not the death of life, but the proof that death is life.

In a nursing home was a veteran of World War I, a very old man. He told me he had been a general, but his records said he had been a captain. "I'm saddled up for the last campaign," he said. He loved that phrase and repeated it each time I saw him. His was the bravado of a little boy playing war games, and the nurse said he kept it up until the end. There are no doubt worse things than going back to childhood at the end, but there are far better things. "Why fear death?" asked Charles Frohman as he went down with the sinking *Lusitania* in 1915. "Death is only a beautiful adventure." Fare thee well, Mr. Frohman. Bravado is an empty echo chamber amplifying the screams of strangled fear.

In sharp contrast to bravado, there is a quiet nobility in the studied dispassion of some of the ancients. Epictetus and other Stoics mastered a disposition of not complaining about or raging against what cannot be helped. Epicurus, on the other hand, went further, suggesting that we do not encounter death at all. "Death is nothing to us; for as long as we are, death is not here; and when death is here, we no longer are. Therefore it is nothing to the living or the dead." One may ask whether this is wisdom or just sophistry. Certainly the living who loved the one who died will think it sophistry, for the death of the beloved is everything to the one who loves.

More common in the history of thought is the idea of the immortality of the soul. The essential person, it is said, is the soul. The soul is temporarily housed in the body and at death is released. The soul uses the body as a musician uses an instrument and sets it aside when the music of life is done. Like a butterfly spreading its wings, the soul at death leaves the chrysalis of the body. Like a sailor stepping out of the boat when it has reached the shore, so the soul leaves the body behind. Among the ancients and in much of Christian thought, these are the dominant motifs. To the other children, Gregory Floyd explains that John-Paul's body is in the ground, but his soul is in heaven. And so it has been said to countless millions in their loss. Surely we should not deny that there is an "I"— call it the soul—that is distinct from, if not independent from, the body. I am, after all, reliably told that every part of the body, down to the smallest molecule, is replaced several times in my lifetime, and yet "I" persist. I have been, as it were, several bodies, but one enduring soul.

I want to insist upon, if you will forgive the awkward term, the "I-ness" of the soul. It is not as though I *have* a soul in the way I have a liver or a kidney. The search for the soul is whimsically caught in these lines from W. S. Merwin's "To the Soul":

> *Is anyone there*
> *if so*
> *are you real*
> *either way are you*
> *one or several*
> *if the latter*
> *are you all at once*
> *or do you*
> *take turns not answering*

That is poetically pleasing, but not, I think, a rewarding line of inquiry. The soul is one with the enduring "I" that embraces, that defines, that gives form to my essential identity—an identity that includes my body. And yet I believe, in a faith disposed toward the future that we call hope, that it endures through its temporary separation from the body.

Today those who make a sharp distinction between body and soul are called "dualists," and it is generally thought a very bad thing to be. Dualism took a more radical turn with the modern era. It is true that Plato and many early Christian thinkers viewed the body as provisional, inferior, and a mere instrument of the soul. Many urged a cultivated contempt for the body and its appetites. But Augustine's anthropology could never have gone along with Descartes's assertion more than a thousand years later: "I have my integrity in being a thinking entity—without body." Descartes was a devout Christian and must not be blamed for everything that would later be called Cartesian, but with that Cartesian turn modern rationalism regressed to a pre-Christian spiritualism. This is a return to Cicero in *Dream of Scipio*: "Be firmly convinced that *you* are not mortal, but only this body." Or Marcus Aurelius in his *Meditations*: "You are a little soul bearing about a corpse." So, again in the nineteenth century, Arthur Schopenhauer exhorts the dying person to greet death as a deliverance: "You are ceasing to be something which you would have done better never to have become. We are at bottom something that ought not to be; therefore we cease to be."

Such a view is not possible for those who know that we are creatures, which is to say we are *created*, which is to say we are meant to be body and soul. In the great tradition of Christian thought, death is all too real. "Of all human evils, death is the worst," says Thomas Aquinas. It is, he said, "the most extreme of all human suffering," in which one is "robbed of what is most lovable: life and being." In the twentieth century, philosophy and theology reacted strongly to the dualism—some call it idealism or spiritualism—of certain rationalistic strains of the Enlightenment. Today it is not at all uncommon to encounter the claims of a radical materialism. The human animal, it is said, is nothing but the body, nothing but physical stuff. There is no soul, and even consciousness is a delusion temporarily sustained by the brain, "a piece of thinking meat" that is wired by neural synapses to process physico-chemical sensations, with the result that we speak, inevitably but self-deceptively, of the existence of "I." From philosophy's immortal soul to science fiction's brain in a vat, human beings have puzzled about the meaning of death, which is to say, about the meaning of life.

In theology, too, especially in Protestant theology of the last century, there has been a sharp reaction against the ancient Greek and later Enlightenment notion of a disembodied mind or soul. Here the turn is not toward materialism—for, after all, God, the ultimate reality, is Spirit—but toward the resurrection of the dead. There can be no doubt that resurrection is absolutely essential to Christian faith. It is as Paul says in 1 Corinthians 15: "If there is no resurrection of the dead, then Christ has not been raised; if Christ has not been raised, then our preaching is in vain and your faith is in vain. . . . Then those who have fallen asleep in Christ have perished. If for this life only we have hoped in Christ, we are of all men most to be pitied."

But we may wonder whether it is the case, as some theologians claim, that belief in the resurrection excludes what is suggested by the immortality of the soul, by the experience of a perduring "I" beyond death. At least I, and many others who have been brought to death's door and back, wonder about that.

FOUR

I F EACH LIFE IS UNIQUE, and it is, then it would seem to follow that each death is unique. I will not dispute the logic of that. And there is no doubt an element of adventure in moving into the unknown. But in my own experience of dying, it struck me as so very commonplace, even trite, that this life should end this way.

Several lawyers have told me my case would make a terrific malpractice suit. All I would have to do is give a deposition and then answer a few questions in court, if it ever came to trial, which it probably wouldn't since the insurance companies would be eager to settle. It would be, I was assured, a very big settlement. The statute of limitations has not run out as of this writing. But I will not sue, mainly because it would somehow sully my gratitude for being returned from

the jaws of death. Gratitude is too precious and too
fragile to keep company with what looks suspiciously
like revenge.

The stomach pains and intestinal cramps had been
coming on for almost a year. My regular physician, a
Park Avenue doctor of excellent reputation, had told
me long ago how pleased he was with the new tech-
niques of colonoscopy. It meant, he said, that none of
his patients need die of colon cancer. His partner, the
specialist in these matters, did one colonoscopy and,
some weeks later, another. After each mildly painful
probing up through the intestines, he was glad to tell
me that there was nothing there. Then, on a Sunday
afternoon, January 10, about five o'clock, after four
days of intense discomfort in which there was yet another probe and yet another X ray, I was at home suddenly doubled over on the floor with nausea and pain.
The sensation was one of my stomach exploding.

My friend George Weigel was visiting, and he
phoned the doctor's office, but the doctor was on va-
cation. The doctor covering for him listened to the
symptoms and prescribed a powerful laxative. (I said
this story would smack of the commonplace.) Much
later, other doctors said that the prescription might,
more than possibly, have been fatal. They said they
never heard of several colonoscopies not detecting a
tumor, and shook their heads over a physician who

would prescribe a laxative after being apprised of symptoms indicating something much more seriously wrong.

Weigel and a member of our community, Larry Bailey, had the presence of mind to bundle me off—pushing, pulling, half carrying me—to the nearest emergency room, which, fortunately, was only a block from the house. The place was crowded. I strongly recommend always having with you an aggressive friend or two when you go to a hospital and are really sick. A large and imperiously indifferent woman at the desk was not about to let anyone jump the line of waiting cases, relenting only when Weigel gave signs that he was not averse to the use of physical violence. She then sat me down to answer a long list of questions about symptoms and medical insurance, which I tried to answer until I fell off the chair in a faint, at which point she surmised she had an emergency on her hands. The experience so far did not instill confidence in the care I was likely to receive.

Very soon, however, I was flat on my back on a gurney, surrounded by tubes, machines, and technicians exhibiting their practiced display of frenetic precision, just like on television. The surgeon who was on duty that night ordered an X ray, which showed a large tumor in the colon, and declared there was no time to lose. I was wheeled at great speed down the halls for an elevator to the operating room, only to discover the elevators were out of order. By then I had been sedated and was feeling no pain. In fact, I was somewhat giddy and recall trying to make a joke about the contrast between the high-tech medicine and the broken-down elevators. A guard showed up who said he knew how to get the number 6 elevator working, and then I was looking up at the white water-stained ceiling of the operating room, and then there was someone putting a mask over my face and telling me to breathe deeply, and then there was "Now I lay me down to sleep . . . ," and then there was the next morning.

The operation took several hours and was an unspeakable mess. The tumor had expanded to rupture the intestine: blood, fecal matter, and guts all over the place. My stomach was sliced open from the rib cage down to the pubic area, and then another slice was made five inches to the left of the navel for a temporary colostomy. I've noticed that in such cases the doctors always seem to say that the tumor was "as big as a grapefruit," but my surgeon insists the blackish gray glob was the size of a "big apple." After they had sewed me up, the hemorrhaging began, they knew not from where. Blood pressure collapsed and other vital signs began to fade. What to do? The surgeon advised my friend to call the immediate family and let them know I would likely not make it through the night.

The doctors debated. To open me up all over again might kill me. On the other hand, if they didn't find and stop the hemorrhaging, I was surely dead.

Of course they went in again. The source of the effusion of blood was the spleen, "nicked," as the surgeon said, in the ghastliness of the first surgery. Given the circumstances, I'm surprised that parts more vital were not nicked. The spleen removed and the blood flow stanched, they sewed me up again and waited to see if I would live. The particulars of that night, of course, I was told after the event. "It was an interesting case," one doctor opined in a friendly manner. "It was as though you had been hit twice by a Mack truck going sixty miles an hour. I didn't think you'd survive."

My first clear memory is of the next morning, I don't know what time. I am surrounded by doctors and technicians talking in a worried tone about why I am not coming to. They kept trying to get me to respond, if even with the slightest sign. I heard everything that was said, and remember feeling vindicated in my having told people over the years to be careful about what they say around patients who presumably do not know what is happening around them. I immediately felt foolish about thinking at such a time whether I was right or wrong about anything. What did it matter? What mattered is that I desperately wanted to respond, but I was locked into absolute immobility, incapable of moving so much as an eye-lash or twitching a toe. The sensation was that of be-ing encased in marble; pink marble, I thought, such as is used for gravestones. The surgeon repeatedly urged me to move my thumb, but it was impossible. My mind was racing, but my body was entirely discon-nected. Perhaps not quite, since I "felt" that my body was there. It had simply stopped taking orders, even the tiniest order that it acknowledge a continuing connection, however slight.

Much later, I read again John Henry Newman's "The Dream of Gerontius," and said, ah yes, it was like that.

> Am I alive or dead? I am not dead,
> But in the body still; for I possess
> A sort of confidence which clings to me,
> That each particular organ holds its place
> As heretofore, combining with the rest
> Into one symmetry, that wraps me round,
> And makes me man; and surely I could move,
> Did I but will it, every part of me.
> And yet I cannot to my sense bring home
> By very trial, that I have the power.
> 'Tis strange; I cannot stir a hand or foot,
> I cannot make my fingers or my lips
> By mutual pressure witness each to each,
> Nor by the eyelids' instantaneous stroke
> Assure myself I have a body still.

Then I heard, "The cardinal is here." It was my bishop, John Cardinal O'Connor. He spoke directly into my right ear, repeatedly calling my name. Then, "Richard, wiggle your nose."

Where did he get that? I wondered. The doctors all wanted me to wiggle my thumb or my toes; he wanted me to wiggle my nose. Probably in Vietnam, I thought. As a navy chaplain, he had been with many at the edge of death.

"Richard, wiggle your nose." It was a plea and a command, and I wanted to do it more urgently than anything I have ever wanted to do in my life. The trying, the sheer exercise of will to wiggle my nose—to order my nose to wiggle itself—seemed to go on and on, and then I felt a twinge, no more than a fraction of a millimeter.

"He did it! He did it!" the cardinal said.

"I didn't see anything," said the surgeon.

So I tried again, and I did it again, and everybody saw it, and the cardinal and the doctors and the technicians all began to exclaim what a wonderful thing it was, as though one had risen from the dead.

The days in the intensive-care unit were an experience familiar to anyone who has ever been there. I had never been there before, except to visit others, and that is nothing like being there. I was struck by my disposition of utter passivity. There was absolutely nothing I could do or wanted to do except to lie there and let them do whatever they do in such a place.

Indifferent to time, I neither knew nor cared whether it was night or day. I recall counting sixteen different tubes and other things plugged into my body before I stopped counting. From time to time, it seemed several times an hour but surely could not have been, a strange young woman with a brown wool hat and heavy gold necklace would come by and whisper, "I want blood." She stuck in a needle and took blood, smiling mysteriously all the time. She could have said she wanted to cut off my right leg and I would probably have made no objection. So busy was I with just being there, with one thought that was almost my one and every thought: "I almost died." I would, in fact, be thinking many thoughts over those days, but they all came back to that one thought: "I almost died."

Astonishment and passivity were strangely mixed. I confess to having thought of myself as a person very much in charge. Friends, meaning, I trust, no unkindness, had sometimes described me as a control freak. Now there was nothing to be done, nothing I could do, except be there. And think about what had overtaken me. I had been outrageously assaulted by this thing growing within me, something entirely alien that had made itself at home and tried to take over. The doctors say they think they "got it all," but of course they do not know, which is why there are tests after tests, and then the chemotherapy, and years before the invader is confidently declared to have been repelled. Yet it is not really an invader; it is something internal to myself. It is a part of myself that went madly wild. What had happened is not the result of weakness or decline, but of an explosion of healthiness—cancer is a healthiness that is radically disordered, that is disengaged from the rest of the body, and therefore deadly in its vibrant aliveness.

Later I would come across Sherwin Nuland's description of cancer in *How We Die*:

> Cancer, far from being a clandestine foe, is in fact berserk with the malicious exuberance of killing. The disease pursues a continuous, uninhibited, circumferential, barn-burning expedition of destructiveness, in which it heeds no rules, follows no commands, and explodes all resistance in a homicidal riot of devastation. Its cells behave like the members of a barbarian horde run amok—leaderless and undirected, but with a single-minded purpose: to plunder everything within reach.

Precisely. Many have spoken of death as an insult, the final indignity that makes a mockery of all our talk about death with dignity. More insulting still that death should raise up as its instrument this band of street thugs in my own neighborhood, my body, and then, insult upon insult, that they should invade through the organ of excretion. Rats scrambling up from the sewer.

Rats, however, are parasites. Not so with cancer. Nuland again: "Its first cells are the bastard offspring of unsuspecting parents who ultimately reject them because they are ugly, deformed, and unruly. In the community of living tissues, the uncontrolled mob of misfits that is cancer behaves like a gang of perpetually wilding adolescents. They are the juvenile delinquents of cellular society." Death was coming not from the outside but from the inside. It was, and it was not, like being hit by a Mack truck. Yes, I had been assaulted, but there was also something within me, inseparable from my "I," that had betrayed me. All these years I had been harboring a traitor. But then I thought again: Perhaps this is not a case of treason; perhaps this is the inexorable working out of something that had been with me from the beginning, from the day I was born toward dying.

Often I had visited the Frick Collection, the most elegant permanent exhibit in the city, and reflected on the Rembrandts, especially the self-portraits. Death and dying are in the pigment; the person is at peace with, or at least resigned to, the terminal consequence of his living. Whether the end comes through a rebellious mob of cancer cells or a tired heart that one day just ups and quits is no matter. It is already there, and the awareness of its presence is evident in the apparent tranquillity of the figure portrayed. Compare with Rembrandt the paintings of Botticelli and the Italian Renaissance. These beautiful people are the immortals. They are untouched, untainted, by mortality. Death can come to them only from the outside, and it must be violent death, for death violates everything that in the vibrancy of life they are. A dagger thrust, perhaps, or poison, but, in whatever form it comes, it is an enemy invader, the antithesis of who and what they are.

In intensive care and, later, hooked up to the machines in my own room, such are the thoughts that fitfully come and go. Death as an intrusive stranger. Death as an intimate acquaintance who had all these years remained in the shadows, but now was stepping forward to claim his due. What is happening is happening to me, but at the same time it is happening within me, and is therefore not separable from what I myself am doing and who I myself am—unless I have nothing to do with my body, which is manifestly not the case. Even when my body was locked in that marble slab and refused to so much as acknowledge my commands, I wanted it to be part of me and, strange as it may sound, I knew it wanted to be part of me. We belong together, my body and I. We have been friends for so long, and the intimacy of communion is so intense, that it is not clear where one begins and the other ends.

A medieval pope, John XXII, got in trouble for teaching that the souls in heaven are not entirely happy, so much do they want to be reunited with their bodies. He said, citing Revelation 6, that the souls in paradise are still "under the altar" and will only be raised to the perfect vision of God (*visio Dei*) when they have their bodies back. After much criticism, Pope John, on his deathbed in 1334, modified his teaching and allowed as how the saints are perfectly happy even before the resurrection of their bodies. But I believe that he had made an important point—that the body is, in fact, essential to the fullness of the self. Given the limitations of our knowledge here on earth, such questions defy completely satisfying resolution, but I was thinking a lot about what is meant by the resurrection of the dead.

Ever so carefully, as he is always ever so careful, Thomas Aquinas addresses the same question in his *Summa Theologica*. More precisely, he does so in Part I of the Second Part, Question 4, Article 5, and he puts the question this way: "Whether the Body Is Necessary for Man's Happiness?" In his usual manner, Thomas first states a long list of objections against answering the question in the affirmative and then offers his reply. In the reply we find this: "For the soul desires to enjoy God in such a way that the enjoyment also may overflow into the body, as far as possible. And therefore, as long as it enjoys God, without the fellowship of the body, its appetite is at rest in that which it has, in such a way that it would still wish the body to attain to its share." So there is nothing lacking in the soul's enjoyment of the beatific vision, but it still desires the body to share the joy. It is just a little like a very happy traveler sending a postcard to a friend, "Wish you were here."

Thomas adds this: "The desire of the separated soul is entirely at rest, as regards the thing desired, since it has that which suffices its appetite. But it is not wholly at rest as regards the desirer, since it does not possess that good in every way that it would wish to possess it. Consequently, after the body has been resumed, happiness increases not in intensity, but in extent." In my own experience, I know that this desirer, anticipating what was ahead, earnestly longed for that increase of extent that would only happen when the "fellowship of the body" was restored. We are not angels. Angels do not by nature have a body, and therefore, says Thomas, in the presence of God "even the lowest angels have every perfection of happiness that they ever will have, whereas the separated souls of the saints have not." Put very simply, there is nothing lacking in the beatific vision, but the perfect enjoyment of that vision awaits the resurrection of the body. So it seemed to me then, and so it seems to me now.

"I almost died." That was the conscious thought, just that little three-word sentence, but those three words were a window into, quite simply, everything. I *almost* died, but in fact did not. Do you only know the thing itself after you have, in fact, died? And then what, if anything, does it mean to "know"? I knew I was dying, in the sense that we are all dying. I thought it possible, and most of the time thought it probable, that I would die very soon. My time has come, my number is up—such banal expressions ran through my mind. But mostly the thought was, "Ah, so this is how it is turning out to be." As with a play, so also with a life, we know it only in retrospect. It is true: In our ending is our beginning. I went back as far as memory would carry me, to when I was young and what I thought, what I hoped, my life would be. What would Richard at age eighteen think of what had happened since? I concluded he would be surprised and, all in all, very pleased. And so Richard, almost half a century later, was, all in all, grateful.

I had long been impressed by those words of John XXIII, the much-loved pope of the Second Vatican Council: "Every day is a good day to be born; every day is a good day to die." I had often claimed, with friends over brandy and a postprandial cigar, that if I died tonight I would say, "Thank you, Jesus." Now it seemed the time had come, and would I say that now? Not so insouciantly as before, yet deliberately, and with a tug of regret about what was not to be that I had expected to be, the answer is yes. I had not planned, I could not have planned, the course of my life up to now; there seemed to be no reason why my plans and expectations should control the final scene. And yet, although I had almost died and thought it more than possible that I was soon dying, the final scene, death itself, was still to come. As others thought they were spectators at my dying, I also was a spectator until called upon to assume my part in the thing itself. This puzzled me: whether dying, the thing itself, is something one can do. Is it an event, is it a deed, or is it something that just happens?

Monsignor Harry Byrne from Epiphany, the church around the corner from the hospital, came to administer Last Rites. Today the sacrament is called the Anointing of the Sick, but the new nomenclature hasn't caught on with most Catholics, just as people still speak of "going to confession" rather than receiving the sacrament of Reconciliation. Father Harry and I have been friends for many years, a friendship marked but not marred by disagreements over his liberal propensities, both political and theological. But this was all priestly business, and he is a priest to his fingertips, a priest of the grizzled, no-nonsense Irish type who does what he is ordained to do and trusts to God that the doing of the thing will do what it's supposed to do. There's a fine Latin phrase for that, *ex opere operato*. Roughly translated, it means the thing works of itself. The sacrament comes with God's guarantee. Don't worry about your feelings or uncertainties or whether you're spiritually fit. Just accept the gift; just accept your acceptance.

Then there was confession, and, yes, I will amend my life if there is a life left to amend, then unqualified forgiveness, for everything, without exception, followed by the anointing with sacred oil and the prayers for healing, if that be God's will, and finally receiving the Body immeasurably more battered than mine, which is called Viaticum, meaning "food for the journey." There now. That just about does it. All the loose ends tied up. It was very straightforward, just as it ought to be. I was drifting into sleep. "Goodnight, Harry. I'll see you." Sometime. Somewhere.

The words of the Last Rites are simple, almost banal. But what the liturgical simplifiers have done to the text cannot completely hide the import of what is being said. Here is the priest in Newman's "The Dream of Gerontius":

> *Proficiscere, anima Christiana, de hoc mundo!*
> *Go forth upon thy journey, Christian soul!*
> *Go from this world! Go, in the Name of God,*
> *The Omnipotent Father, who created thee!*
> *Go, in the Name of Jesus Christ, our Lord,*
> *Son of the Living God, who bled for thee!*

Go, in the Name of the Holy Spirit, who
Hath been pour'd out on thee! Go, in the name
Of Angels and Archangels; in the name
Of Thrones and Dominations; in the name
Of Princedoms and of Powers; and in the name
Of Cherubim and Seraphim, go forth!
Go, in the name of Patriarchs and Prophets;
And of Apostles and Evangelists,
Of Martyrs and Confessors; in the name
Of holy Monks and Hermits; in the name
Of Holy Virgins; and all Saints of God,
Both men and women, go! Go on thy course;
And may thy place today be found in peace,
And may thy dwelling be the Holy Mount
Of Zion—through the Same, through
    Christ, our Lord.

But I did not go, not yet. If you linger, you might receive the Last Rites several times, and I did. After a
while, if it appears you might be coming back, the
prayers for the commendation of the dying give way to
the accent on the healing, and the Viaticum is understood as food for the continuing journey here on earth.
In those first days and weeks, however, my thoughts
were entirely about moving on. If death is to be now,
let it be now. Yet there was that puzzlement. I could
not conceive what it is to die. To be dying—I knew
about that. That we are born toward dying, that opinion was divided as to whether or not I was near that final point—I knew about that. But to die, the thing

itself, that I was trying to understand. I am returned to "Now I lay me down to sleep."

As a boy in my attic bedroom I could at times see the moon through the dormer window. Again and again, I determined to keep my eyes on the moon and so stay awake in order to experience the actual moment when I went to sleep. I wanted to know, to witness, the event of passage from the state of being awake to the state of being asleep. But of course I never succeeded in this quest. There was the experience of being awake, and then of being sleepy and heading into sleep; there were dreams that I knew were dreamed while sleeping, and then the experience of waking up and looking back on the undoubted fact that I had been asleep. Sleepiness was experienced as a thing within me moving toward sleep and, at the same time, a thing outside me that overtook and overcame me. This, I thought, was surpassingly strange. When did I, from within me, go to sleep? When did it, from outside me, overtake me? Where am I, or am I at all, when I am sleeping? Of course there was nothing original in my childhood ponderings. Anthropology offers many accounts of cultures that weave wondrous tales about the mystery of sleep. But on my hospital bed I saw again, in my mind's eye, the moon through the attic's dormer window and wondered more deeply about the moment of going to sleep, the moment of dying.

FIVE

SINCE THEN, I have gone back to reread philosopher Josef Pieper's wise little book *Death and Immortality*. He claims that "even in violent, 'non-natural' death, whose cause may be an accident, an infection, a proliferation of cells, or a crime—even then the death takes place simultaneously from within, as the result of life, as the last step of a way initiated at birth, as an act of the dying person himself." As an act of the dying person himself? Perhaps so, but as I lay dying I could not get my mind around that. I thought, for instance, of the person committing suicide. Is it really true that he kills himself, or does he only do the thing that precipitates death killing him? Is one thing happening, or two things? Is there one acting agent, or two? At eighty miles per hour, with one jerk of the steering wheel, someone crashes into a concrete barrier, or someone pulls a trigger, sending a bullet into the brain, or leaps from a bridge. There is the act, and then there is the dying itself.

Pieper writes, "And in that dying there is not only a blow from outside, but at the same time an action, an act proceeding from the personal center and terminating life from within, an act by which the life attains to the result intended from the start." Perhaps so. Recall Rembrandt's portraits of those dying from within, and Botticelli's beautiful young people who could only be killed from without.

Through the centuries, Death has been personified, sometimes as the Grim Reaper, who comes to keep a foreordained appointment that cannot be rescheduled. It then seemed to me, and it now seems to me, that there is a strong element of truth in that imagery. Just as so long ago in my attic bedroom I was overtaken and overcome by sleep. As insistent, however, is the thought that I act in going to sleep. And so I lay there thinking both that I am dying and that death is coming for me. It is tempting to seek escape from the conundrum in simple cause-effect explanation. Cancer is the cause, and being dead is the effect. That is the viewpoint of the outside observer: There is a disease, and then there is a corpse. But I am not an outside observer. This is happening to me! Between the familiar state of living toward death, now arrived at mortal illness, and the state of being dead, where am "I"?

As I said, for long times I was utterly passive, especially in the intensive-care unit. They could have done anything to me. What was it to me? The probing, cutting, puncturing, siphoning—they were doing it to my body, an exhausted bag of bones and blood and guts in which they seemed to have a great deal more interest than I did. At least at the moment, out of sheer weariness, I was almost ready to let the body go. Let them do what they want with it. For the most part, I was not in pain. Anyway, pain and discomfort were irrelevant; these people were going to do what these people do, and I had little or nothing to say about it.

A defense of sorts was to indulge in a certain ironic distancing. I remembered a college classmate—I'll call him Woody—who had a most peculiar relationship to his body. After working up a sweat on the baseball field, he would say, "I'm going to give it a shower." At night he said, "I think I'll put it to bed," and on the way to the cafeteria, he said, "It's really hungry. I hope they don't have meat loaf again. It hates meat loaf." I'm sure he wasn't trying to be funny. He talked that way all the time. He was a world-class dualist. There is, no doubt, a label for that in the diagnostic manuals of psychiatry, severe dissociative cognition or something of the sort. Whatever it is called, it comes in handy when you are dying and need a rest from wondering about how to locate the "I" and the "me," the subject and the object of what is happening.

Death may be experienced as the final letting go of everything, body and spirit. *In manus tuas commendo spiritum meum*—"Into your hands I commend my spirit." At any other time—when going to sleep, for instance—there is a qualifying clause; at some point you are going to take your spirit back. Not this time. This time is for keeps. When you are dying you have to do something with yourself, and since there is very little you can do about yourself, the only thing to do is to give yourself away. It is something like a surrender, but not unambiguously so. To call it a surrender may be a face-saving ploy; your self is being taken from you, so you say you are surrendering yourself. You can adopt that skeptical view, and in fact I did adopt it at times, but I also resisted it. I resisted it because I also knew the wrenchingly wonderful truth that I *was* surrendering myself. Here again I encountered the troubling entanglement of love and death. Love at its most profound is the gift of the self. But who will receive such a gift and, having received it, what will they do with it?

When you are very sick, you are intensely aware of the reactions of others. The doctors, the nurses, the nurses' aides, they accept the surrender, indeed they assume it. But, with exceptions, you are to them not a person, but a case; you have surrendered to them not your self, but your condition. It is foolish to resent their cool professionalism. They need it as an emotional buffer. To be sure, there were times when I wished a nurse, or even the young woman who changed the sheets, knew how cherished was a believable word of personal caring, but in the hospital one does not expect much in terms of what is called meaningful relationships. The staff are set upon completing their rounds, and necessarily so. I surrendered myself to them, but only in the general sense that they represented the world of the hospital that had so suddenly displaced my world.

It is with friends from my world that I became intensely aware of reactions. With some, and not always the closest of friends, the gift of self, or at least the fact of my helplessness, was readily received. It did not surprise me that these were usually women. They seem to be more at home with helplessness. With others, usually men, there was an obvious nervousness that I might give them something; not my sickness, but something deeper that they wouldn't know how to handle, that they didn't want to learn how to handle. There was no end of visitors during the weeks in the hospital and the long months of coming back at home. In the hospital, when dying seemed imminent, I noted the reactions most acutely. It was not said, but more than once I imagined someone thinking: "He is dying and I will go on living. He is giving me a piece of his dying self, and I don't know what to do with that." There was a distancing, a recoil, in visits paid that were but paying the dues of friendship. I did not resent that. I, too, had dutifully stood at the beds of the dying eager to get away untouched by death.

In manus tuas commendo spiritum meum. But into whose hands? Into the hands of God, of course. But God created us for human community, and that community is not limited by death. John Donne's poetic insight that no man is an island is the wisdom of who we are and how we are with one another. Love is the gift of the self, and the gift may be unwanted. My dying, I thought, is a letting go, and those around me who are within the orbit of love must make a decision about picking up what is let go. I know I am saying this awkwardly. Here is an untitled poem of July 1915 by Anna Akhmatova. She says an important part of what I am saying so poorly.

He didn't mock me, he didn't praise,
As friends would have done, and
    enemies.
He only left me his soul
And said: Look after it.

And one thing troubles me:
If he dies now,
God's archangel will come to me
For his soul.

How then will I conceal it,
Keep it a secret from God?
This soul, which sings and cries,
Ought to be in His paradise.

"Look after it." There were many who were look-ing after me. But later on, when I am gone and the looking after me is done, look after it. Look after this life that was, this life that is surrendered, that is com-mended into your hands because your hands were there. This life may be, please God, in his paradise, but it is also here with the human community from which and for which he brought it to be in the begin-ning. And now in my ending I looked at those around my bed. "Into your hands . . ." And some said yes.

After the two surgeries, when they went in once for the cancer and then opened me up again to find and stanch the hemorrhaging, in the early hours of the morning George Weigel called my brothers and sisters. They should come if they wanted to see me alive, just barely, but Mim must come in any event. She is the firstborn, and she takes charge in family crises. I am ashamed to say that I was not surprised to find her here. It is the sort of thing she does. I expect it is a general truth that, when we are very sick, we tend to take others for granted. I am sure I said many times— many times, but not times enough—that I was sorry to be such a bother, but I'm afraid I meant it only a little more than half. After all, a dying patient—and, later, a recovering patient who almost died—is entitled. That is a terrible thing to think, and I am not sure I thought it in just those words, but the assumption, the presumption, was there.

Much later, Mim let me see the journal she kept during those days. When George called her in Pensacola, she did not want to come. Her husband, Luther, was just my age when, a few years earlier, he died after two surgeries for colon cancer. She agreed to come, but "all the time I was praying that Richard would be out of intensive care by the time I got there." She dreaded facing the IVs, the tubes, the catheter, the plugs, the respirator, the transfusions, the bleeping monitors—in short, the replication of Luther's dying.

Many years earlier, she had been through all that with their infant Tommy who, after two surgeries, lived on machines for several days before he died. It was too much for Mim, but she came. One day after I was out of intensive care, a nurse was changing the bandages and exposed the entirety of my stomach. I gazed with fascination at this deep red ditch running from chest to groin, with a tributary veering leftward to the colostomy. Mim was there, too, and she blanched at seeing again what last she had seen of Luther's body, a day before he died.

The very sick can look simply awful. Although they politely tried to hide it, I saw the recoil on the faces of visitors. A young parishioner arrived unannounced and, before I knew what she was doing, started snapping pictures. Now I'm glad she did. I came across the photos again the other day. I looked nothing short of ghastly, a corpse awaiting the undertaker's makeup. Little wonder that people think they would rather be dead than lying there so pitifully and humiliatingly destitute of any capacity for life. But they are wrong about that. I do not want to say that it was not so bad, but a little life goes a long way. As we have all the time there is, so also, as long as we are alive, we have all the life there is. There is the cliché that while there is life there is hope, but I do not mean that. At times I had little hope that I would ever be well again. I mean, rather, that while there is life there is life, as much life as there ever was. I suppose I do want to say that it was not so bad. It was not so bad as it looked.

But that was only after I got over the embarrassment and the humiliation of the circumstance. Here I lay, stripped of all appearances and all pretense. As Lear said of Poor Tom on the stormy heath: "Is man no more than this? Consider him well. Thou owest the worm no silk, the beast no hide, the sheep no wool, the cat no perfume. Ha! Here's three on's are sophisticated; thou art the thing itself; unaccommodated man is no more but such a poor, bare, forked animal as thou art." That's about it. Unaccommodated man. The thing itself. Take a long look. But I am still alive with all the life there is.

Please do not misunderstand. I did not think such things, much less say them, in a mood of defiance. Defiance was the farthest thing from my mind. It was simply the embarrassment and humiliation of being exposed for what I am, the thing itself. One afternoon I opened my eyes to see that a dear friend, a protégé in fact, had come to visit. He would not look at me, at this ghastly pallor, this blasted body, with not enough strength to even raise my hand. He was embarrassed for one he had looked up to and admired, and I was embarrassed. There came to mind one of the most humiliating moments of my life. I was in kindergarten and suddenly during recess I had the most urgent need to relieve myself. Running from the playground, I almost made it to the bathroom, but only almost. I shuffled back to class, head hung low, face red with shame, pants dripping wet. And so I said to my friend who was standing by the hospital bed, "Don't be afraid to look. I've wet myself all over." I'm sure he didn't know what I was talking about, and I did not have the energy to explain. But at some point we are all Poor Tom. Unaccommodated man. The thing itself. To lie there dying was not so bad, once I got over the embarrassment of it.

Hospitals infantilize their patients, or so it is said. I wouldn't have minded a little infantilizing, if that was the price to be paid for getting care that was a bit more caring. There were, to be sure, nurses straight out of central casting; starched, officious, and given to saying "we" when they meant me. "It's time for our beddy-bye," said one each night when she turned out the light. I thought that the prospect of beddy-bye with her held no enticement. Then, too, hospitals today have support staff to help you with emotional and psychological adjustments. The day came when I was to be trained to take care of the colostomy. This is a messy business of handling excretions through a hole in the side of the stomach. After demonstrating the mechanics of the thing, an imperious middle-aged woman with an impressive Irish brogue explained that having a colostomy would likely lower my self-esteem and I might therefore want to join a support group called "Colostomates."

It had come to this. I, who had until yesterday, or so it seemed, been esteemed as a person of consequence, a priest, a writer, an editor, a lecturer, a sought-after consultant to institutions dedicated to setting the world aright, I should go to meetings to share with others my problems in coping with the nasty stuff excreting into a plastic bag attached to my belly. She had no idea what she had done to my self-esteem. Poor unaccommodated man. The thing itself.

Of course I did not sign up for "Colostomates." There is this, though: Like most healthy people, I had always been bored to distraction by the sick and old chattering endlessly about their operations and medications. During those weeks and months, I discovered that, when you are really sick, a more entrancing subject can hardly be imagined. The world turns around aches and pills, and did you hear that there is a drug you can get in Canada to counter the nausea from chemotherapy? Moreover, patients form conspiracies for and against doctors. After a while, I could get out of bed and, holding on to the wheeled pole with the feeding tubes and other paraphernalia, stumble down the hall where I met with other stumblers to talk about who did what to whom.

I was, all in all, fortunate in my doctors. There was the surgeon, who went in without delay, even if there was that mishap with the spleen, requiring him to open me up again. We have remained friends in the years since. My primary-care physician, as they are called, thought the surgeon, like most surgeons, was a "cowboy" who did more cutting than was necessary. He, on the other hand, was a student of Hegel. He sat with me by the hour as the chemo slowly dripped into my arm and talked about history, consciousness, and the World Spirit. I wanted to talk about whether I had another six months to live. Then there was the oncologist, a pleasant gentleman of high repute. (You soon discover that almost everyone has a doctor who is one of the top two or three, if not the very top, in his field.) He had a marvelous command of fine, almost metaphysical, distinctions regarding which treatments just possibly might—and to what degree they just possibly might—have a bearing on which outcomes. We had fascinating conversations about my physical well-being in relation to my other states of being. I called him my ontologist. In the end, at the urging of others who had gone through horrors in prolonged chemotherapy, I chose the shortest course possible, entrusting my ontological destiny to higher authority.

I have not mentioned a most curious part of the story, and readers may make of it what they will. Much has been written on "near death" experiences. I had always been skeptical of such tales. I am much less so now. I am inclined to think of it as a "near life" experience, and it happened this way.

It was a couple of days after leaving intensive care, and it was night. I could hear patients in adjoining rooms moaning and mumbling and occasionally calling out; the surrounding medical machines were pumping and sucking and bleeping as usual. Then, all of a sudden, I was jerked into an utterly lucid state of awareness. I was sitting up in the bed staring intently into the darkness, although in fact I knew my body was lying flat. What I was staring at was a color like blue and purple vaguely in the form of hanging drapery. By the drapery were two "presences." I saw them and yet did not see them, and I cannot explain that. But they were there, and I knew that I was not tied to the bed. I was able and prepared to get up and go somewhere. And then the presences—one or both of them, I do not know—spoke. This I heard clearly. Not in an ordinary way, for I cannot remember anything about the voice. But the message was beyond mistaking: "Everything is ready now."

That was it. They waited for a while, maybe for a minute, maybe longer. Whether they were waiting for a response or just waiting to see whether I had received the message, I don't know. "Everything is ready now." It was not in the form of a command, nor was it an invitation to do anything. They were just letting me know. Then they were gone, and I was again flat on my back with my mind racing wildly. I had an iron resolve to determine right then and there what had happened. Had I been dreaming? In no way. I was then and was now as lucid and wide awake as I had ever been in my life.

Tell me that I was dreaming and you might as well tell me that I was dreaming that I wrote the sentence before this one. Testing my awareness, I pinched myself hard, ran through the multiplication tables, and recalled the birth dates of my seven brothers and sisters, and my wits were vibrantly about me. All of this took five or seven minutes, maybe less. I resolved at that moment that I would never, never let anything dissuade me from the reality of what had happened. Knowing my skeptical self, I expected I would later be inclined to doubt it. It was an experience as real, as powerfully confirmed by the senses, as anything I have ever known. That was some seven years ago. Since then I have not had a moment in which I was seriously tempted to think it did not happen. It happened—as surely, as simply, as undeniably as it happened that I tied my shoelaces this morning. I could as well deny the one as deny the other, and to deny either I would have to play very peculiar tricks with my mind.

"Everything is ready now." I would be thinking about that incessantly during the months of convalescence. My theological mind would immediately go to work on it. They were angels, of course. *Angelos* simply means "messenger." There were no white robes or wings or anything of that sort. As I said, I did not see them in any ordinary sense. But there was a message; therefore there were messengers. Clearly, the message was that I could go somewhere with them. Not that I must go or should go, but simply that they were ready if I was. Go where? To God, or so it seemed. I understood that they were ready to get me ready to see God. It was obvious enough to me that I was not prepared, in my present physical and spiritual condition, for the beatific vision, for seeing God face to face. They were ready to get me ready. This comports with the doctrine of purgatory, that there is a process of purging and preparation to get us ready to meet God.

I should say that their presence was entirely friendly. There was nothing sweet or cloying, and there was no urgency about it. It was as though they just wanted to let me know. The decision was mine as to when or whether I would take them up on the offer.

In Newman's dream, his guardian angel (do I have two guardian angels?) hands him over with these words:

> Now let the golden prison ope its gates,
> Making sweet music, as each fold revolves
> Upon its ready hinge. And ye, great powers,
> Angels of Purgatory, receive from me
> My charge, a precious soul, until the day,
> When, from all bond and forfeiture released,
> I shall reclaim it for the courts of light.

Perhaps that is what my visitors were prepared to do for me.

I said that I then and there resolved never to doubt what had happened. That does not mean that I have not subsequently questioned it. I have done so many times. There is that marvelous statement by Newman that a thousand difficulties do not add up to a doubt. I believe that. A doubt is a decision against something. You tell me that something happened or that you are going to do something, and I say, "I doubt that." That is a decision against. It is a very different matter if I say that I do not understand how that happened or how you are going to do what you promised to do. That means I have a difficulty with what you are telling me, but a thousand difficulties do not add up to a doubt. Difficulties occur in a search for understanding. In the case of what you are telling me, I am disposed to believe that what you are saying is true, although I do not understand how it can be.

That what I remember happening that night *really* happened is not an article of faith for me—and certainly not an article of faith for anyone else. To speak of what we can know about what *really* happened is to step into the deep mires of that department of philosophy called epistemology. As it is not an article of faith, so also my remembrance of what happened is not a philosophical certitude. But I have reported what I remember, and remember very clearly. I expect the experience best belongs in the category of what the Christian spiritual tradition calls a "consolation"— a comfort and support in times of distress and danger. The Christian tradition in its wisdom is very cautious about such experiences. Although we are encouraged to exuberance of faith, we are warned against unbridled enthusiasms and spiritual sensationalism. The great danger is in confusing such an extraordinary experience with an article of faith, and then, if it turns out to be delusory, one may face a crisis of faith with respect to teachings grounded in revealed truth and backed by clear and public reason.

It is settled doctrine among almost all Christians that *public* revelation ended with the apostolic era. But after the first century God did not go out of the business of communicating with his creatures. Over the centuries, numerous saints of impeccable orthodoxy have reported such communications, often in the form of apparitions or visitations. Thus, at least for Catholics, the apparitions of the Blessed Virgin Mary at Lourdes, Fátima, Guadalupe, and elsewhere. These are commonly called private revelations, although they can have great public repercussions in the devotions that grow up around them. If such events do not contradict what is known from public revelation and is formally taught by the Church, if they are reinforced by other events of an apparently miraculous nature, and if the resulting cult enhances faith and strengthens the faithful, the Church may encourage such devotions. But it is not an article of faith that, for instance, Bernadette Soubirous did actually, in the summer of 1854 outside the village of Lourdes, see Mary and receive messages from her. Without going into all the reasons for thinking so, I, along with millions of others, think she did. The most commonly encountered argument against thinking so is that such things do not happen, which is simply an assertion and no argument at all.

What happened to me on that hospital bed was, of course, no world-class apparition. There was no message to be conveyed to anyone else. It was a word very personally addressed to me. To judge from what many others say, it was not even so extraordinary, at least not in terms of the frequency of such things happening. More than a third of adult Americans say that they have at some point in their lives received communications from angels, saints, or God himself, and, at least on the surface, many reports bear similarities to mine. I cannot judge such reports, although, as I said, I am skeptical about some of the more elaborate and apparently fanciful accounts of "near death" experiences. Nor am I forgetting that a third of the population—not necessarily the same third—believes in the sightings of UFOs. That is quite beside the point. Unlike the existence of UFOs (about which I have no experience or judgment whatever), I am firmly convinced, on the basis of sound reason, of the existence of angels, although I expect they are a great deal more mysterious than is suggested by their representation in the cartoons of the popular imagination.

But I continue to have difficulties with what I so clearly remember. It was so unambiguously benign, suggesting such a smooth and easy transition between this life and whatever is to follow. That does not fit my understanding of the wrenching and painful separation of soul from body, the destruction of the body-soul being that I am. But then, that separation had not happened; presumably I had not yet died; the experience was on the near side of death. Then too, the Christian tradition, along with Plato and the best of the ancients, insists that death is followed by judgment, a final reckoning. That is a prospect that is not unattended by fear, even terror. Yet the message was so very friendly and consoling, as though a positive outcome of the judgment was confidently anticipated. This raises a dramatically different possibility. As there are good angels, so there are evil angels. What if this visitation was in fact a temptation to presumption, to the mortal sin of taking for granted the mercy of God? At least hypothetically, that cannot be ruled out. But I do rule it out, for all this happened in the context of conscious and firm reliance on the forgiving grace of God in Christ.

But again, did it *really* happen? And does it really matter whether it *really* happened? Both questions are important. Perhaps I was hallucinating—even hallucinating about the mental gymnastics I went through to prove to myself that I was not hallucinating. After all,

I was under some sedation, it was night, and I had been sleeping. How could such a putative experience be falsified? Perhaps if there had been an objective observer watching me at the time who saw me sleeping, who could testify that I did not sit up in bed, did not open my eyes, and only later on, when I woke up, did I report having had such a vision. Then I probably would have said that I had a very strange dream, and that would be that. Or maybe not. Unless one subscribes uncritically to the materialist dogma that dreams are entirely and without remainder caused by physico-chemical functions of the body and its brain, there is the possibility of communications from elsewhere through dreams. There is venerable philosophical, as well as biblical, precedent for giving credence to that possibility. Critical credence, to be sure, but credence nonetheless.

There are visions that we generate and visions that we receive, and no clear rule for telling the one from the other. It may be that in visions we touch upon realities of which what we call reality may be only the shadowland. Dostoyevsky wrote:

There are moments, and it is only a matter of five or six seconds, when you feel the presence of the eternal harmony. . . . A terrible thing is the frightful clearness with which it manifests itself and the rapture with which it fills you. If this state were to last more than five seconds, the soul could not endure it and would have to disappear. During these five seconds I live a whole human existence, and for that I would give my whole life and not think that I was paying too dearly.

The eternal harmony manifests itself, he writes. It fills you. It is a vision received.

Of course, Dostoyevsky was an epileptic, and today's neuroscience might suggest that his visions could be "cured" by minor surgery on the brain. Perhaps so, but here we are returned to the materialist claim that mind and consciousness and visions—in a word, the soul— are all delusional. There is no doubt that a laser beam or scalpel operating on parts of the brain can alter consciousness, as there is also no doubt that my thinking demonstrably alters the operation of the brain. Meditate on God and the infinite, evoke an erotic fantasy, worry about a forthcoming exam, or attend fully to Bach's *Mass in B Minor,* and the monitoring machines show the most complex excitements produced in the activity of the brain. Which "causes" which?

The manipulation of the brain affects mental activity and, just as surely, mental activity affects brain activity. Did my brain cause me to meditate on the infinite, or did my decision to meditate on the infinite enlist the brain in the service of my meditation? I say that I decide to listen to the *Mass in B Minor,* but maybe what I call my deciding is no more than an event dictated by a neural synapse in my brain. But is it the case, then, that my brain dictates and decides things? For instance, does it decide that I am now deciding that that is not so? Go very far in that direction and we begin to speak about the brain as though it had a soul; maybe that it is a soul; maybe even that it is what we mean when we speak of *the* soul. But we know that that is not what we mean by the soul. Certainly it is not what I mean by the soul. It is not what I mean by *my* soul. I just this minute once again decided that. And if someone claims that it would be more accurate to say that my brain produced the event that I call deciding, I have to make a decision about that, too; and so it continues in infinite regress until we are back in the perfect circle of solipsism that keeps college-dormitory bull sessions going late into the night.

Recall Pascal's *pensée:*

> Man is only a reed, the weakest of nature; but
> he is a thinking reed. . . . And should the
> universe trample him, man is even more noble

than what kills him, because he knows he is
dying, and the universe knows nothing of the
advantage the world has over him. All our
dignity consists in thought. It is in thought that
we must elevate ourselves, and not in space and
time, which we cannot fill.

The tramplings of matter and of materialistic doctrine cannot extinguish the dignity that alone under-
stands what is happening. Taking their cue from Pascal, some have contended that it is in our knowing the
tragedy of bodily death that bodily death is deprived
of its final tragedy. Perhaps so.

In 1974, the philosopher Thomas Nagel published a
wonderful essay, "What Is It Like to Be a Bat?" The essay is great fun in its convoluted complexity, and it has
generated many other essays over the years, both
agreeing and disagreeing with Nagel's argument. In trying to understand the connections between body,
brain, mind, and consciousness, Nagel counters the
materialists (he calls them physicalists) by insisting that
we concentrate on what we mean by the phenomenon
we call "experience." An experience—such as the experience of being a bat—is necessarily subjective. What is
often passed off as the "scientific" approach, however,
strives to be objective. Objectivity aims at the universal

that transcends the particular. The problem is that, precisely as we try to be objective about experience, our attention moves away from what we want to be objective about, namely, experience, which is necessarily subjective. Nagel puts it this way: "If the subjective character of experience is fully comprehensible only from one point of view, then any shift to greater objectivity—that is, less attachment to a specific viewpoint—does not take us nearer to the real nature of the phenomenon: It takes us farther away from it."

As I say, such arguments are endlessly fascinating. But of this I am persuaded: Between brain and thought, between matter and spirit, there is a wondrous correlation for which the right word is "mystery." It is a correlation akin to what Thomas Aquinas termed the "fellowship" between body and soul, a fellowship that is temporarily sundered by death. And might there not also be, in visions, a fellowship between soul and soul that death cannot sunder? I do not know how it can be reasonably denied. Certainly my brain did not then, and does not now, direct that I deny it. Round and round I went, looking at it from this angle and that, and thus did I arrive, and thus do I remain, at the point of critical credence.

But my thinking about what happened that night did not stop there. Also included in the skeptic's catalogue of difficulties is the possibility that I simply mis-remember what happened. That is very unlikely, how-ever, since in the hours, days, and weeks following the event I was going over and over the details. Were I mistaken in my recalling of what happened, it would be a mistake without parallel in my experience. There is no rational excuse for crediting such a hypothetical possibility. So do I think it happened as I remember it happening? Yes. Is the interpretation I have placed upon the experience accurate? It seems to me the most plausible interpretation. It makes most sense of what happened. Am I glad it happened? Yes, glad and grate-ful. It is an abiding consolation and, in its remem-brance, an ever recurring occasion to recognize that reality is ever so much more strange than we are in-clined or able to imagine. Such a thing has not hap-pened to me since. It is enough.

I do not wish to be misunderstood. With this expe-rience, as remarkable as it was, and with all these reflections, I do not suggest that I have "explained" anything about death and dying. Death eludes expla-nation; death is the death of explanation. The many dimensions of dying are evident in the everyday ways we speak of it and in the experience of the dying. Leave out any one dimension, and the result is a false account. But include every dimension that we can imagine, and one still does not have an adequate account. "Death is a natural part of life," we are told. That trite statement, intended to rob death of its strangeness and terror, is, I am sure, false. Life is not adequate to death. Life includes dying, but life does not include death.

We speak of death as an ending and as a transition to something else. It is the terror of destruction, and it is liberation. Death attacks from without and matures from within. It is both violent alien and a friend's offer of peace beyond understanding. Death happens to us without our permission and invites our collaboration. It is the most natural of things and the destruction of everything that is natural and right. Little wonder that the poets never tire of the subject. In dictionaries of quotations, the number of entries on death is second only to the number of entries on love; the one, like the other, seeming to be everything and nothing, the more indescribable as it is the more described.

I do not say that death cannot be anticipated. After all, there are the saints who have gone to visit in paradise and returned to tell us about it. Or so it is claimed. The great twentieth-century theologian Hans Urs von Balthasar, a man of towering intellect and rigorous sobriety, wrote hundreds of pages at the dictation of his friend Adrienne von Speyr as she reported on her visits to heaven. Is it possible that death is part of life, after all, or even that death is not at all? Is it possible that, between this world and the next, we simply move from life to life? Adrienne von Speyr did not, according to the accounts, have to die in order to go to heaven and back. I do not pretend to understand this. I know what I understood by the announcement to me that night. If I chose to go with them, something would happen between here and where we were going, and that something is called death. I did not take that next step. Had I taken it, I sensed that I would be moving into the unknown, into what I could not anticipate in advance.

Montaigne wrote a famous essay, "To Philosophize Is to Learn to Die." I do not believe that. I believe that one learns to die not by philosophizing, but by dying. In his *Dialogue of the Carmelites*, set to the wondrous music of Poulenc, Georges Bernanos has the prioress, who is getting ready to climb the scaffold, say, "I have meditated on death every hour of my life, but that does not help me at all now." In the Great Terror of the French Revolution, the sisters who had been arrested by the revolutionary tribunal marched to the guillotine singing an improvised hymn to the tune of the *Marseillaise*, declaring that their execution was to be their *jour de gloire*, their day of glory. Before mounting the steps, each sister kissed the small statue of the Madonna and Child held by the prioress; then each asked her, their religious superior: "Permission to die, mother?" And the prioress said, "Go, my daughter." And then at last it was the turn of Mother Teresa of St. Augustine. "I have meditated on death every hour of my life, but that does not help me at all now." Whether it helped her in the very last instant, God only knows.

In another sense, the question may be beside the point. To meditate on death is to meditate on a helplessness that we only know in dying. "That does not help me at all now." Nothing *we* can do can help now. That is the point.

SIX

E VERYTHING IS READY NOW." Had I then and there said yes, the next step would have been the moment of truth. Truth undoubtable and irrevocable. From Socrates and Plato through the entirety of the humane tradition, a secure belief has been that a verdict will be rendered upon the life concluded. And in that last moment is an instance of perfect freedom in which one is asked to submit to judgment. I say again that I did not fear the judgment. Perhaps that is presumption, perhaps an unwavering faith in the mercy of God. That, too, is for God to judge. It is simply that the message did not require that the judgment be now. It could be delayed for a time. In that, too, I was granted freedom. I was given permission to think it over for a time. Or so I understood the message.

It would mean leaving my body behind, for clearly that devastated body with all its tubes and wires and clamps wasn't going anywhere. That was a sadness, since I was very attached to my body. Well, I thought, this body would be going to an undertaker, probably to the one around the corner on Second Avenue. I had long ago made up my mind that I did not want to be embalmed. A funeral Mass the next day and then into the ground to await the resurrection, that's the way I wanted it. I mentioned this to a priest friend who told me it would not be possible. The cardinal, he explained, insists upon presiding at the funeral of every priest and often he is in Rome or otherwise prevented from getting there for several days. So embalming it is, then. I know it sounds odd, but I thought I owed my body an apology for this further and egregious indignity.

Which brings us back to the idea of death as the separation of soul and body. The notion of some of the ancients and the Enlightenment rationalists that the essential "I" is not involved in the death of this body struck me as preposterous. It is this body that was washed in the waters of Baptism, that has received times beyond numbering the Body of the crucified and risen Jesus, that was anointed with the sacred oils in ordination and the final Viaticum. It is this body, now in pitiful ruins, that participated in the yearnings of my loves, the bracing joy of early morning walks, the holding of Albert as he died, and all those nights of languorously falling into sleep. Not to mention the sounds of Mozart and the taste of a surprisingly fine Merlot at the Italian restaurant up the street. The body remembers. Even my thinking is sensuous; as I lay there going back in memory my recollections are tactile, touching the burlap of disappointments and running my fingers over the velvet of joys recalled. This body and I, this body that is inseparable from me, together we have been this life. That medieval pope was right. And Thomas Aquinas was right. No matter what the joy of the beatific vision, I think, it will not be perfect until my body and I are together again. Or, put differently, heaven will be perfect, but I, body and soul, will not be perfectly present to the perfection until then.

Thomas again: "The soul united with the body is more like God than the soul separated from the body, because it possesses its nature more perfectly." God is Spirit, and therefore one might think that the soul, which is spirit, is more like God when divested of the physical encumbrance that is the body. But, no, we are most like God when we are most what we are by nature, which is to say, when we are most fully what God created us to be, and God created us to be soul and body. We are embodied souls, some say, while others prefer to say we are ensouled bodies. In fact, we are soul and body. To truly say "I" is to say, at the same time, soul and body. I do not claim that I thought this through in quite this way as I lay there pondering the visitation of that night. But I have been thinking about it ever since, and bit by bit it becomes more clear, even obvious.

While I rested at home, about a month after the visitation and before the third surgery, an evangelical Protestant friend came by to see me, and we were soon deep into the discussion of these matters. It is neither necessary nor possible to understand these things, he objected. It is enough to believe the words of Jesus to Martha in John 11: "I am the resurrection and the life; he who believes in me, though he die, yet shall he live, and whoever lives and believes in me shall never die."

Well, yes, there is nothing deficient in the words of Jesus. They are enough and more than enough. But what does it mean when we say that we believe what he says? Believing and understanding cannot be separated; they can be distinguished, but they cannot be separated. The classic definition of theology, which applies to all our thinking about what we believe, is "faith in search of understanding." In any event, the undeniable fact is that I cannot *not* think about what the words of Jesus might mean. I am living, I believe in him, and he says I shall never die. But I almost died a month ago, and I am certainly going to die—probably, it seems, sooner rather than later. I'm sorry, but I do Jesus no favors by saying that I believe something that has every appearance of being contrary to fact.

So we are returned to the question of body and soul and how we locate the "I." My friend says that is not very original, to which I say, So what? Socrates, Plato, Paul, Augustine, Aquinas, Teresa of Avila, and a thousand other worthies have pondered these questions at great length, and I'm supposed to have something original to say? However stumbling my thoughts, the subject has been rather suddenly and rudely pressed upon me in terms of *my* body and *my* soul. The question has attained, one might say, a certain existential urgency. There is no question that this body is dying. The question is the immortality of the soul. At least that is the way it is usually put, but here I take a leaf from the aforementioned philosopher Josef Pieper and recast the question in terms of the *indestructibility* of the soul. Talk about the immortality of the soul plays too easily into the hands of radical dualists, idealists, gnostics, romantics, and rationalists—from ancient Greece to contemporary science fiction—who suggest that the body is accidental to the soul. In this view, the essential "I" is unaffected by the death of the body. There is an unseemly pride, indeed hubris, at work here: "I am made of the eternal stuff, the divine stuff, which can never die." Thus do we imagine that we are gods.

It is very different with the indestructibility of the soul. Here it is unblinkingly recognized that death is a destruction. Death is a catastrophic severing of body and soul, a destruction of the self who is by nature body and soul. That I am both body and soul is confirmed by my entire life experience. My soul—or consciousness, or animating spirit, or self, call it what you will—is not just incidentally attached to my body. My dying body cries out to me that it is mine, that I cannot let it go and still be fully "I," that we are together, and only together are we this one life actually lived—this one life of which it was said, "he who lives and believes in me shall never die." Yet my body is undeniably dying. On Ash Wednesday, with the imposition of the cross on the forehead, "Remember, O man, that you are dust and to dust you shall return." Goodbye, dear body. Off you go to the undertaker, to the earth, to the maggots, to the dust.

I suppose it is possible that someone reading this is a student of philosophy, and maybe a student of Scholastic philosophy at that. Such a reader may be thinking that I am using the term "soul" rather loosely, and he or she would be right. Yes, I know that, in the strict philosophical sense, the soul is not a being, never mind a thing, but the principle of being whereby a person in time and space and body is brought to perfection, even to a knowledge of the mystery of God. I do not wish to dispute any of that, but this is not a philosophical seminar. I am reflecting on what I thought and felt—often confusedly, even contradictorily—as I lay dying. These are snatches of philosophy, theology, biography, poetry, and heaven knows what else, all churning, as I discovered them churning, around the question of what was happening to the me I call "I." There are, it seemed to me at times, more answers to that than the Bundren family had answers to the question of who was Addie, the dead wife and mother, as they took her to the graveyard in Faulkner's *As I Lay Dying*.

And so it was that I thought of myself bidding this body farewell. But who or what is this that is left to say good-bye? Call it the soul. It has survived the catastrophe of death; it is indestructible. Through the centuries, many philosophers and theologians have offered "proofs" in support of the immortality of the soul. Some of these proofs are intended to establish the probability of the soul's survival; others claim to be knock-down arguments that establish the matter beyond all reasonable doubt. Here is what I kept thinking about—sometimes in a muddle and sometimes with almost frightening lucidity—as I lay dying, and especially after that strange visitation. I kept thinking that there is a *truth* about things, a truth that I know, however inadequately, and the truth, if it really is the truth, cannot die. Please stay with me here, for it is not an easy path of thought on which I found myself.

Here is the crucial connection: The truth is indestructible and the soul is capable of apprehending the truth. Freud wrote, "In the unconscious each of us is convinced of his own immortality." Freud himself did not think that this fact is probative, as the lawyers say—it does not serve to prove the truth of what people are convinced of. On the other hand, he thought it a very important fact about human beings. He did not simply mean that, in opinion polls or surveys, most people say they believe in immortality. In his considered judgment, based on careful observation, everybody believes, in the preconscious dimension of their psychic life, that they are immortal. If that is true, it may not prove anything, but it is very much worth thinking about.

Josef Pieper writes, "One may very well wonder if all people . . . should without exception be able to deceive themselves in regard to so fundamental an existential matter as 'immortality.'" Well, yes, at least theoretically it is surely possible that all people deceive themselves, especially when we have a strong interest in wanting to believe something that isn't true. And the fact is that many thoughtful people insist that they do not believe in immortality. They say that brain, mind, consciousness, and "soul" are all totally depend-

ent upon the body and die when the body dies; and
the body does undeniably die. It will not do simply to
claim that such people really do believe what they say
they do not believe. We must not cheat here. Although people could be deceived in believing that the
soul is indestructible, it is also true that nobody wants
to be deceived. Not really. A person may say that he
"prefers" to think that something is true, which means
that he hopes it is true. I cannot imagine a person
hoping that what he hopes is true is not true. In other
words, nobody wants to be deceived. So Pieper has a
point. If Freud is right in saying that, at the very deepest level, all people are convinced that they are immortal, that should be given more weight than Freud
himself gave it. But I do not think it "proves" the indestructibility of the soul.

As I was trying to make sense of what was happening to me, body and soul, my mind was flooded with
thoughts about the connections between matter and
spirit. For years I had been reading about, and even
doing some writing about, the debates over the relationship between brain, mind, and consciousness.
These are endlessly complex and fascinating debates,
as we saw in connection with Thomas Nagel's argument in "What Is It Like to Be a Bat?" They engage related questions having to do with Einstein and relativ-
ity theory, and how mass and energy are not separate

realities. Beyond Einstein, and in some ways against him, they engage theories about quantum jumps in which the line between matter and energy (or spirit) seems to be almost obliterated. The more we know about the strangeness of reality, the more the old dualisms that pitted body against soul and matter against spirit seem impossibly simplistic. These considerations entered into the conversation, so to speak, between my body and my soul.

Yet I kept being drawn back to the point about truth, how it is indestructible and how the soul is able to apprehend it. Thomas Aquinas said that the angel and the human soul are imperishable, *incorruptibiles*, because they are by nature capable of grasping truth, *capaces veritatis*. What does it mean, I asked myself, that the soul has a capacity for truth? This presupposes, of course, that there is such a thing as truth. Everyone knows that today there are many who think it is clever to deny that. They say, in effect, "There is no such thing as truth, and that's the truth." Anyone involved in serious questions, such as those about life and death, will give short shrift to such sophistry. "What is truth?" Pilate asked Jesus, in cynicism or despair. Many today think Pilate's question is the mark of a sophisticated mind. In fact, we all assume, we cannot help but assume, our capacity for truth. Every act of speech assumes that a truth has been recognized, or at least it assumes the ability to recognize truth. I later came across this in Pieper: "Speaking means to make reality recognizable and to communicate it. And truth is nothing but reality's being known."

Truth is reality's being known. Certainly my physical senses inform my thinking, and my thinking involves my brain. Both physical senses and brain are part of the body. If my body dies, and therefore physical senses and brain stop functioning, is there an "I" who still knows the reality I knew? Presumably, the reality that I knew continues after I die. But maybe not. After all, the reality that I knew included the "I" who knew it. It is one thing when it comes to relatively simple physical realities. That table across the room will, I thought, still be standing there pretty much as it is after I die. I know there are some who claim that the reality of the table will be significantly affected by the withdrawal of the energy field of my being, but that strikes me as verging on science fiction, or at least venturing beyond what can be known, or, at the very least, moving beyond what I can understand. It is a quite different thing, however, when it comes to the reality of personal relationships. This took me by surprise: The more I thought about these matters, the more the conceptual gave way to the personal.

The truth that is the reality known in personal relationships, and especially in the most important relations with others, necessarily involves the contin-uation of the "I" beyond my death. Such a relation-ship does not simply come to an end; it does not sim-ply disappear. Minimally, "I" continue to be a reality in the consciousness of the other. This is more, I thought, than the cliché that we live on in the mem-ory of others. I will be more than a memory, some-thing recalled, with ever increasing difficulty, from the past. To the extent that my life has significantly influenced the life of another, I continue to be part, in myriad ways of which the other person may not even be conscious, of the living of that life. The other per-son is aware of me not simply as a memory, but as a presence. The more difficult question is whether I will be aware of myself being present to that person.

But at this point I drew back from the edge of a quicksand into which many have wandered and sunk. Spiritualist experiments with seances and communica-tions "from the other side," which have fascinated so many, held absolutely no interest for me. Not that I deny that such things are possible. I am grateful that, al-ready as a child, I was introduced to the strangeness of reality. In catechism class, for instance, we were taught that the Witch of Endor really did conjure the spirit of the dead prophet Samuel at the command of King Saul. Such things were possible, they happened, but it was also very wrong to toy with such happenings. That is flirting with the dark powers, with evil. That is what I was taught, and that is what, upon a lifetime's reflection, I still believe. To be sure, there are smart people who do not believe in the reality of evil. As for me, a knowledge of history, of others, and especially of myself puts the reality of evil beyond reasonable dispute. As important in my drawing back from the edge of the quicksand of spiritualism, however, is that I had no desire to hang on or hang around. With death, this life in space and time was over. If there was life after the catastrophic sundering of body and soul, it seemed to me obvious that that life, that "I," had to be a moving on to something else.

So I kept coming back to this *capaces veritatis*—the soul's capacity for truth. A more Thomistic philosopher than I am—Josef Pieper, for example—could put it in the form of a syllogism. It might go like this: Because the human soul is capable of apprehending truth as such; because it is capable of this act which by its essence goes beyond every conceivable material contingency and remains independent of it; because, thus understood, it is capable of an *operatio absoluta*—therefore it must also have an *esse absolutum*; it must possess a *being* independent of the body; it must be an entity that persists through the dissolution of the body and beyond death.

That is very persuasive, but not, I think, conclusive. The weakness, it seemed to me, is in the second step, what is called the minor premise. What if the materialists are right who say that the very consciousness of apprehending truth is totally dependent upon the body, and especially the brain? When the brain ceases to function, all consciousness of apprehending truth dies with it. Is there a soul without consciousness of itself? That struck me as very doubtful, to say the least. One might think that we will all find out in due course whether or not the materialists are right. But of course we won't because, if they are right, there will be no "we" to find out anything. In any event, I am not a materialist and, as I say, I found the syllogism persuasive. I thought its conclusion to be true. But it was not conclusive in the sense of being a knock-down argument, an irrefutable proof, against all possible objections by a reasonable person.

The more I thought about it, the more I became convinced that the *capaces veritatis* must be understood in more personal terms. In John 14, Jesus says, "I am the way, and the truth, and the life." This was a passage that bore in upon me with irresistible strength during those weeks and months. I had personally apprehended Jesus, who is the truth. More important, I had been personally apprehended by him. I knew him. He knew me. I readily admit that this certainty depends upon the fact of Jesus being risen from the dead. As Paul writes in Romans 6, "Christ is raised from the dead never to die again; death has no more dominion over him." Of course there are many who think the resurrection of Jesus an eminently debatable question. Suffice it to say that I had long ago come to the conclusion that the resurrection of Jesus is the only convincing explanation of the evidence we have. To explain how I came to that conviction would be a subject for another book. It is enough here to say that I have never seriously wavered from that conviction.

Moreover, there is a personal relationship of apprehending and being apprehended. I could no more deny that relationship than I could deny myself, for it is utterly formative of who I am. That is the way it is with personal relationships of deepest consequence. Consider the relationship between a husband and wife who have been lovingly married for forty years, and how the "I" of the one is inseparable from the "I" of the other. The two are, in biblical language, one flesh. Consider that, and then go even deeper to the possibility of a relationship that is, so to speak, one soul. Another passage that had always been important to me now became my constant companion. It would not let me go. In Galatians 2, Paul writes, "I have been crucified with Christ: the life I now live is not my life, but the life which Christ lives in me; and my present mortal life is lived by faith in the Son of God, who loved me and gave himself up for me."

In the years before my sickness, I had written about this passage in terms of "the transposition of the ego." That still seemed to me a good phrase. Christ had taken my life into his, and I had taken his life into me. There was, as it were, an exchange of essential identities. But now it seemed to me to be much more than a good theological point. Now it was the absolute center of what was happening to me, and what was going to happen to me. It was the crux—the cross point. This is what Christians mean when we say that in Baptism we die and rise again with Christ. This is what we mean when we say that we have been crucified with Christ, that on the cross he offered up not only his life, but our lives as well.

And thus it became luminously clear to me as I fitfully puzzled through these questions, lying there on the hospital bed: I have already died! My death is behind me! The question of what is to happen to me now is not a question about me, but a question about Christ. And that question has been answered. "Christ is raised from the dead never to die again; death has no more dominion over him." Therefore death has no more dominion over me. At some point "it" will happen. This body will be separated from this soul, and that is a great sadness. I was not expecting it so soon. I would have, all things considered, preferred to go on as I had been for many more years. But it did not really matter that much. The old difficulties came back from time to time. What if I am deluded about Christ and his death and resurrection? But the difficulties were more a nuisance than a threat, and a thousand of them could not add up to a doubt. I remember thinking that I could more easily have doubted my own existence, although I'm not sure I would want to defend that proposition in a philosophical seminar.

As I was saying good-bye to my body, this thought, too, pressed upon me: In the great reunion that is the resurrection of the dead, will we recognize one another, my body and I, my body that is part of who I am? We are told that when Jesus appeared to the disciples after his resurrection, he was changed; they did not recognize him; they thought he was a ghost. But then he showed them his wounds, where the nails of the cross pierced his hands and his feet, where the sword cut into his side. The glorified Jesus was recognized by his wounds. So also would I know my body by its wounds, the wounds we received in our long life together. Here also I was not being original, but only thinking the matter through for myself. The first Christians puzzled through these questions as well. We know that because Paul speaks to their puzzlement, as, for instance, in this hymnlike passage from 1 Corinthians 15:

But some one will ask, "How are the
  dead raised? With what kind of
  body do they come?"

You foolish man! What you sow does
  not come to life unless it dies.

And what you sow is not the body
  which is to be, but a bare kernel, perhaps
  of wheat or of some other grain.

But God gives it a body as he has chosen,
  and to each kind of seed its own body. . . .

What is sown is perishable, what is
  raised is imperishable. It is sown in
  dishonor, it is raised in glory.

It is sown in weakness, it is raised in
  power. It is sown a physical body,
  it is raised a spiritual body.

If there is a physical body, there is
  also a spiritual body.

Thus it is written, "The first man
  Adam became a living being"; the
  last Adam [Christ] became a life-
  giving spirit. . . .

The first man was from the earth, a
  man of dust; the second man is
  from heaven. . . .

*I tell you this, brethren: flesh and
    blood cannot inherit the kingdom of
    God, nor does the perishable inherit
    the imperishable.*

*Lo! I tell you a mystery. We shall not
    all sleep, but we shall all be changed,
    in a moment, in the twinkling of an
    eye, at the last trumpet. For the
    trumpet will sound, and the dead
    will be raised imperishable, and
    we shall be changed.*

*For this perishable nature must put on
    the imperishable, and this mortal
    nature must put on immortality.*

*When the perishable puts on the
    imperishable, and the mortal puts
    on immortality, then shall come to
    pass the saying that is written:*

"Death is swallowed up in victory."

*"O death, where is thy victory?
    O death, where is thy sting?"*

*The sting of death is sin, and the
    power of sin is the law.*

*But thanks be to God, who gives us the
    victory through our Lord Jesus Christ.*

At the beginning and at the end, and then at every step along the way, it became evident that this matter of what was in prospect for me engaged concepts and theories and doctrines, but most commandingly it turned on the personal: What had happened with Christ would happen, was happening, with me. His death and his life anticipated my death and my life. This realization breaking through was a breaking out of all my puzzlings and ponderings about the destiny of this elusive "I."

Cogito ergo sum, said Descartes. Yes, perhaps so, but as certainly—no, more certainly—*Cogitor ergo sum.* "I am thought, therefore I am." I have been taken into account, and, in being taken into account, have been brought into being and am sustained in being. In the destiny of Christ is my destiny; and so it had been all along, and so it would be forever. This, too, broke through: That, when I die, in his Body, the Church, of which I am part, and in his Body in the Eucharist, which this body has received times beyond numbering, body and soul are already reunited, however imperfectly. What is now imperfect will one day be perfected in resurrection. The maggots should enjoy me while they can; they will not have the last word. Mortal dust already stirs with its longing for that great reunion. So he promised, and so I came to believe more surely than I had ever believed before. Faith in search of understanding was not yet satisfied, but neither was it disappointed.

SEVEN

W E ARE COMING near the end now, for there is not much more to tell. There is this, however, about being really sick: You get an enormous amount of attention. I cannot say that I did not enjoy it. In the pain and the nausea and the boredom without end, there were times when I was content to lie back and enjoy the attention. It was a kind of compensation. Over these days there were hundreds of cards and letters and phone calls and, later, brief visits—the last by people who sometimes betrayed the hope of having a final word with what they took to be their dying friend. Some of those who checked in I had not seen in years. Nor have I seen them since, so busy are we with our several busynesses. Sickness is an enforced pause for the counting up of our friends, and being grateful.

In all the cards and letters assuring me of prayer, and almost all did offer such assurance, there were notable differences. Catholics say they are "storming the gates of heaven" on your behalf and have arranged to have Masses said. Evangelical Protestants are "lifting you up before the throne." Mainline Protestants, Jews, and the unaffiliated let it go with a simple "I am praying for you" or "You are in my prayers." One gets the impression that Catholics and evangelicals are more aggressive on the prayer front. Mim took a phone call and could not at first understand the heavy Italian accent on the other end. It was the papal nuncio relaying a message from the pope that he was praying for me. In her diary she wrote, "I hope Richard is not going to get a big head from all this attention."

Then there were longer letters laying out the case for my getting better. A friend who is a constitutional scholar at an Ivy League university wrote a virtual lawyer's brief summing up the reasons for dying and the reasons for living, and came down strongly on the side of my living. It was very odd, because after that there were a number of similar letters, all arguing that I should stay around for a while and assuming that I was undecided about that. I was undecided. But I was not afraid, and this struck me as strange. At the time of crisis and in the months of recovery following, I was never once afraid.

Many years earlier, I think while I was still in college, I came across these lines by J. V. Cunningham:

> *An old dissembler who lived out his lie*
> *Lies here as if he did not fear to die.*

I very much liked that, perhaps because, in its curmudgeonly way, it cut through the cant of Whitmanesque insouciance in the face of dark truths, a smug cant I have always found repellent. I typed out Cunningham's lines on a three-by-five card and pinned it to the wall. I still have that card, now yellowed with age, and I still like those lines for the same reason I liked them before. But when it seemed my time had come, I did not fear to die. About that I was quite sure I was not dissembling.

I do not claim my not being afraid as a virtue; it was simply the fact. It had less to do with courage than with indifference. Maybe this is "holy indifference," what the spiritual manuals describe as "a quality in a person's love for God above all that excludes preferences for any person, object, or condition of life." Aquinas, St. John of the Cross, and Ignatius of Loyola all write at length about such holy indifference. All I know is that I was surprisingly indifferent to whether I would live or die. It probably had less to do with holiness than with my knowing that there was nothing I could do about it one way or the other.

As to the ardor for life that people talk about, how much of that is put on? And maybe the putting on is so convincing as to generate something like ardor. I thought about Niel, the raw young Midwesterner who was brought out, as they say, by the ardent Mrs. Forrester of Willa Cather's *A Lost Lady*. In a fine piece of writing that seemed aimed at challenging my indifference, Cather has Niel looking back many years later on the woman who had disillusioned him by her wayward love:

He came to be very glad that he had known her, and that she had had a hand in breaking him into life. He has known pretty women and clever ones since then—but never one like her, as she was in her best days. Her eyes, when they laughed for a moment into one's own, seemed to promise a wild delight that he has not found in life. "I know where it is," they seemed to say, "I could show you!" He would like to call up the shade of the young Mrs. Forrester, as the witch of Endor called up Samuel's, and challenge it, demand the secret of that ardour; ask her whether she had really found some ever-blooming, ever-burning, ever-piercing joy, or whether it was all fine play-acting. Probably she had found no more than another;

but she had always the power of suggesting things much lovelier than herself, as the perfume of a single flower may call up the whole sweetness of spring.

About the source of the will to life, about the ardor for life, I have known those who seem to say, "I know where it is. I could show you." Usually they are women. Women know more than we men about the natural springs of living beyond existence. One risks interminable arguments today in making any generalization about the differences between the sexes, but I do think that women know more because they become pregnant and give birth, because there are those long months when they cannot help but ponder the beginning of life, and therefore the end of life, and therefore life itself. And because they have fewer delusions about being in control and are the stronger for it. I speak at least of women I have known. They wanted to will me to life, and I am grateful for that; but I was shattered, and it seemed to me that the shattering must go deeper still if I was to be changed as I must be changed.

On the other hand, there was the message: "Everything is ready now." As though the decision were mine to stay or to go. A friend sent me a card with those words from the meditations of Pope John XXIII, this time in Italian, *Ogni giorno e buono per nascere; ogni giorno e buono per morire*—"Every day is a good day to be born; every day is a good day to die." That also rang true. How is it possible that so many different, even conflicting, emotions can coexist? To be shattered, and at the same time to be indifferent, tranquil, almost insouciant about what is happening and what is going to happen. As a young man in 1963 I listened to radio accounts of the slow dying of Pope John. It was announced one day that he was offering his sufferings on behalf of the hungry of the world, the next day on behalf of prisoners, the next on behalf of unborn children. And so it went from day to day. He was going about his dying with a kind of craftsmanship, putting his dying to good use, wasting nothing.

In his journals, John XXIII had frequently quoted the description of another saint: "He neither feared to die nor refused to live." On May 31, 1963, after the stomach cancer had taken its toll, the pope's secretary, Monsignor Loris Capovilla, fulfilled a promise he had made long before, telling him, "Holy Father, I am now performing the same duty you performed for Monsignor Radini at the end of his life. The hour has come; the Lord is calling you." The press was informed, and, as a friend who attended the final Mass in St. Peter's Square below the apartment where the pope was dying put it, "It seemed that the whole world gathered in a vigil around his deathbed." The Mass began at seven on the evening of June 3, and when it ended at seven-forty the huge crowd joined in singing *Ubi caritas et amor ibi Deus est*, "Where charity and love are, there is God." Above in his room, where the hymn could be heard, John XXIII trembled for an instant, and then peacefully died.

I imagined that in those days before the end, maybe his body, too, was pierced with needles and tubes, and I imagined him examining them and dedicating each one to some good purpose, as he recalled St. Paul's words to the Colossians, "Now I rejoice in my sufferings for your sake, and in my flesh I complete what is lacking in Christ's afflictions for the sake of his body, that is, the church." Not, of course, that there was anything deficient in Christ's suffering, but he allows us to have a share in his redeeming work, which can only be done through suffering. The idea is very beautiful, and not morbid at all.

I understood the theology involved, and I tried to make the piety mine, but with limited success. *Ogni giorno e buono per morire*. Yes, but is this the day, or are there to be many more days, perhaps even years? I puzzled at myself puzzling over whether the decision was mine. "He neither feared to die nor refused to live." This psychological double, this "I" that was watching me, was bemused to discover that I agreed with me that it was all so very uncertain: whether the decision was mine, and what the decision should be if it really were mine to make.

Another friend had written with his son the story of his son's several years of waging heroic battles against a horrific series of cancers. He sent me their book, inscribed with the admonition "to fight relentlessly for life." It was very kind of him, but I was not at all disposed to fight. More to the point were those letters calmly laying out the reasons why it would be better for others, if not for me, were I to live rather than to die. Over the slow weeks and slower months of recovery, I gradually came to agree. But still very tentatively.

When I was recuperating at home and could take phone calls, those calls became a staple of everyday existence. There were dozens of calls daily; closer friends called every day. Somebody was always on call-waiting. I enjoyed it shamelessly. Although I was often too tired to talk, when I had the energy I related in detail, over and over again, every minuscule change in my condition. With a credible display of intense interest, people listened to the problems with colostomy bags and the latest wrinkle in controlling the nausea that came with chemotherapy. And always in my talking, I was on the edge of tears. I, who had seldom cried in my adult life, was regularly, and without embarrassment, blubbering. Not in sadness. Not at all. But in a kind of amazement that this had happened to me, and maybe I was going to die and maybe I was going to live, and it was all quite out of my control. That was it, I think: I was not in charge, and it was both strange and very good not to be in charge.

Tentatively, I say, I began to think that I might live. It was not a particularly joyful prospect. Everything was shrouded by the thought of death, that I had almost died, that I may still die, that everyone and everything is dying. As much as I was grateful for all the calls and letters, I harbored a secret resentment. These friends who said they were thinking about me and praying for me all the time I knew also went shopping and visited their children and tended to their businesses, and there were long times when they were not thinking about me at all. More important, they were forgetting the primordial, overwhelming, indomitable fact: We are dying! Why weren't they as crushingly impressed by that fact as I was?

After a month or so, I could, with assistance, walk around the block. *Shuffle* is the more accurate term, irrationally fearing with every step that my stomach would rip open again. I have lived in New York almost forty years and have always been a fierce chauvinist about the place. When you're tired of London, you're tired of life, said Dr. Johnson. I had always thought that about New York, where there is more terror and tenderness per square foot than any other place in the world. I embraced all the clichés about the city, the palpable vitality of its streets, the electricity in the air, and so forth and so on. Shuffling around the block and then, later, around several blocks, I was tired of it. Death was everywhere. The children at the playground at 19th Street and Second Avenue I saw as corpses covered with putrefying skin. The bright young model prancing up Park Avenue with her portfolio under her arm and dreaming of the success she is to be, doesn't she know she's going to die, that she's already dying? I wanted to cry out to everybody and everything, "Don't you know what's happening?" But I didn't. Let them be in their innocence and ignorance. It didn't matter. Nothing mattered.

Surprising to me, and to others, I did what had to be done with my work. I read manuscripts, wrote my columns, made editorial decisions, but all listlessly. It didn't really matter. After some time, I could shuffle the few blocks to the church and say Mass. At the altar, I cried a lot and hoped the people didn't notice. To think that I'm really here after all, I thought, at the altar, at the *axis mundi*, the center of life. And of death. I would be helped back to the house, and days beyond numbering I would simply lie on the sofa looking out at the back yard. That birch tree, which every winter looked as dead as dead could be, was budding again. Would I be here to see it in full leaf, to see its leaves fall in the autumn? Never mind. It doesn't matter.

When I was a young man a parishioner told me, "Do all your praying before you get really sick. When you're sick you can't really pray." She was right, at least in large part. To be sure, there is a kind of prayer in all the fretful thinking about what had happened, was happening, and was going to happen. The pondering and puzzling was always in the awareness of the Presence. But being really sick—vomiting, and worrying about what will show up on the next blood test, and trying to ignore the pain at three o'clock in the morning—is a full-time job. Most of the time, you want to recede into relatively painless passivity and listen to your older sister reading Willa Cather, as my sister read to me. During those long nights, *My Antonia, Death Comes for the Archbishop, Shadows on the Rock,* and at those times I could have wished it to go on and on. Not that it mattered, but it was ever so pleasant being ever so pampered.

As I said earlier, people are different around the very sick, especially when they think they may be dying. In the hospital, bishops came to visit and knelt by my bedside, asking for a blessing. A Jewish doctor, professing himself an atheist, asked for my prayers with embarrassed urgency. His wife had cancer, he explained, "And you know about that now." Call it primitive instinct or spiritual insight, but there is an aura about the sick and dying. They have crossed a line into a precinct others do not know. It is the aura of redemptive suffering, of suffering "offered up" on behalf of others, because there is nothing else to be done with it and you have to do something with it. The point is obvious, but it impressed me nonetheless: When you are really sick it is impossible to imagine what it is like to be really well; and when you are well it is almost impossible to remember what it was like to be really sick. They are different precincts.

I had lost nearly fifty pounds and was greatly weakened. There was still another major surgery to come, to reverse the colostomy. You don't want to know the details. It was not the most dangerous surgery, but it was the third Mack truck, and for a long time afterward I barely had strength to lift my hand. Then, step by almost imperceptible step, I was recovering and dared to hope that I would be well again, that I would stride down the street again, that I would take on new projects again. Very little things stand out like luminous signposts. The first time I was able to take a shower by myself, it was like dying and rising again in baptismal flood. When one day I was sent home from the hospital after another round of tests, I was told that, if I did not urinate by five o'clock, I should come back to the emergency room and someone would put the catheter back in. My heart sank. It was quite irrational, but going back to the emergency room would have been like recapitulating the entire ordeal of these last several months. I could not endure the thought. When at four o'clock I peed a strong triumphant pee, my heart was lifted on high, and with tears of gratitude I began to sing with feeble voice a Te Deum. I thought, "I am going to get better." And I allowed myself, ever so tentatively, to be glad.

Others were more certain than I that I was recovering. For the first time in my life I noticed that people were saying things like, "You're looking so well." I recalled the old saw that there are five stages in life: childhood, youth, adulthood, middle age, and "You're looking so well." But these people seemed to mean it. The truth, the embarrassing truth, is that I felt a certain resentment about their rushing my recovery. Didn't they know I was still teetering between life and death? Some people appeared to be in an unseemly hurry to drop the curtain on my drama.

Only two weeks after the third operation, Cardinal O'Connor asked me to say Mass with him at the cathedral and then join him for breakfast. It was my first venture out of the neighborhood, and I undertook it with considerable trepidation. The conversation went on for a long time. He talked about securing the future of my ministry, because he might not be around very long and then there would be another bishop who "knew not Joseph." (As it happened, he was my bishop for another seven years.) I was grateful for his caring, but the conversation struck me as unreal. It seemed to me then very uncertain that I had enough of a future to worry about.

Only later, and at first grudgingly, did I admit to myself that maybe I was holding on to my sickness. Nobody said that I was, but it was obvious that others saw in me more health than I felt and thought it was time to move on. To this day, I am not sure that I was entirely wrong to hold on for a while, if that is what I was doing. The encounter with death, I thought, had not changed me as much as it should have. I must stay with this for a while longer, in order to understand what happened, in order to understand what I learned about myself and my relation to the ultimacies of life and death. I suppose my writing about it now is part of my staying with it. It will always stay with me.

That was seven years ago. I feel very well now. They tell me I might be around for many more years. Medical science, perhaps arbitrarily, says five years is the point of complete recovery when you are reassigned to your age slot on the actuarial chart. But just to be safe, the tests continue on a regular basis. Next Monday we get the latest report on the CEA (carcinoembryonic antigen), the blood indicator of cancerous activity, although the doctor says the test is really unnecessary. But I think I am well now. It took a long time after the surgeries, almost two years, before the day came when I suddenly realized that the controlling thought that day had not been the thought of death. And now, in writing this little book, it all comes back. I remember where I have been, and where I will be again, and where we will all be.

There is nothing that remarkable in my story, except that we are all unique in our living and dying. Early on in my illness a friend gave me John Donne's wondrous *Devotions upon Emergent Occasions*. The *Devotions* were written a year after Donne had almost died and then lingered for months by death's door. He writes, "Though I may have seniors, others may be elder than I, yet I have proceeded apace in a good university, and gone a great way in a little time, by the furtherance of a vehement fever." So I too have been to a good university, and what I have learned, what I have learned most importantly, is that, in living and in dying, everything is ready now.